A LEAP OF FAITH

Into an Ongoing Adventure with God

A LEAP OF FAITH

Into an Ongoing Adventure with God

Bob & Joan Galasso

Pleasant Word

© 2005 by Bob and Joan Galasso. All rights reserved

Pleasant Word (a division of WinePress Publishing, PO Box 428, Enumclaw, WA 98022) functions only as book publisher. As such, the ultimate design, content, editorial accuracy, and views expressed or implied in this work are those of the author.

No part of this publication may be reproduced, stored in a retrieval system or transmitted in any way by any means—electronic, mechanical, photocopy, recording or otherwise—without the prior permission of the copyright holder, except as provided by USA copyright law.

Unless otherwise noted, all Scriptures are taken from the Holy Bible, New International Version, Copyright © 1973, 1978, 1984 by the International Bible Society. Used by permission of Zondervan Publishing House. The "NIV" and "New International Version" trademarks are registered in the United States Patent and Trademark Office by International Bible Society.

Scripture references marked KJV are taken from the King James Version of the Bible.

Scripture references marked NASB are taken from the New American Standard Bible, © 1960, 1963, 1968, 1971, 1972, 1973, 1975, 1977 by The Lockman Foundation. Used by permission.

ISBN 1-4141-0457-X
Library of Congress Catalog Card Number: 2005925320

Dedication

We dedicate this book to God, our Abba Father who continues to lavish His love on us.

>...to bestow on them a crown of beauty instead of ashes, the oil of gladness instead of mourning, and a garment of praise instead of a spirit of despair. They will be called oaks of righteousness, a planting of the Lord for the display of His splendor.
>
> (Isaiah 61:3)

>Nothing is lost when Jesus Christ walks into your life and touches your broken heart. All that died or was crushed in your soul is brought to life and by His touch and His direction will bring much fruit and bless many lives.
>
> (Joan C. Galasso)

Table of Contents

Dedication v
Foreword ix
Introduction xiii

Chapter 1: An Invitation 15
Chapter 2: Working Harder 21
Chapter 3: What Went Wrong? 31
Chapter 4: Too Little Too Late 41
Chapter 5: Coming Apart at the Seams 49
Chapter 6: Lessons Learned 59
Chapter 7: The Freedom of Boundaries 71
Chapter 8: Joy Restored 77
Chapter 9: Beauty for Ashes 89
Chapter 10: Starting Over 97
Chapter 11: Back to School 109
Chapter 12: Summer Struggles 115
Chapter 13: God's New Call 123
Chapter 14: A Leap of Faith 135
Chapter 15: Lord, What Is Our Mission? 151

Chapter 16: On the Road Again 161
Chapter 17: Satisfied 175
Chapter 18: A Renewed Passion 187
Chapter 19: An Ongoing Adventure 195
Chapter 20: Now It's Your Turn 203

Endnotes 211

Foreword

In Revelation 3:8, the Lord says,

I know your deeds. See, I have placed before you an open door that no one [no man, no woman, no thing] can shut. I know that you have little strength, yet you have kept My Word and have not denied My Name.

But what do you do if after walking through that door your little strength becomes no strength? What if you have tried so hard to do everything right—to be all things to all people—that at last, you are broken and utterly spent physically, mentally, emotionally and spiritually?

Bob and Joan Galasso walked through the "open door" in 1973 as they entered the ministry. In a short fifteen years, after being an area director with youth for Christ, a youth pastor, church planter and a senior pastor working full steam ahead 24/7, the Lord allowed Bob and Joan to be brought to a screeching halt. Suffering from clinical depression and burnout in 1988 both would experience the wonderful healing power of God.

I have personally known Bob and Joan Galasso since 1985. Each of them has had a tremendous impact on my family and me. We witnessed first hand the work of the Holy Spirit as both sought to serve Him with all of their hearts. We have been privileged to see the awesome Hand of God deliver them through the valley of brokenness and back into the brightness of His Glory.

In Psalm 18:2 where it states, "the Lord is… my deliverer," it becomes vital to understand the full impact of the word *deliver*. It means several things. First, it means to be set free from, to carry away to safety, to cause to escape. Second, deliver or *paw-lat*, also means to give birth to or to act as a midwife for. Third, deliver in the root meaning is to send forth by discharging, to throw a blow. In His perfect plan for Bob and Joan's lives, our loving Lord caused them not only to experience His healing deliverance *from* their brokenness, they were also delivered *to* the new chapter in their lives. There, God has grown and fitted them to be prepared for the third and final work; to be *sent forth*, discharged by the Deliverer to deliver His Word to the rest of hurting humanity with a brand-new anointing and fresh power from on high.

Their story is a marvelous account of how God not only kept the door opened but utterly transformed their lives in order to prepare them for the richest ministry yet—to bring the healing power of God to the hurting. Perhaps in your own life, *you* have known pain or exhaustion or brokenness. Be encouraged as you read the Galasso's real and relevant story that God is no respecter of persons. In Jeremiah 31:3 we find these words, "The Lord appeared to him from far away. I have loved you with an everlasting love; therefore, I have continued my faithfulness to you."

Foreword

The word love is *aw-hab* meaning an intense affection for, to feel love for, to have a passionate attraction and enthusiasm for. Passionately, just as enthusiastically as our Lord in His love set about delivering Bob and Joan, He cares and is concerned for you. That this book has come into your hands is a divine appointment with our God. For what He has so graciously done for the Galasso's, He lovingly waits to do for you. As you read this book, join Bob and Joan in experiencing a Leap Of Faith.

by Marci Young

Introduction

The story you are about to read is true. However, it is actually a "tale of two stories." Each of the stories comes out of the brokenness of heart and life of its main characters. You see it is a tale of two people who came to realize they had a problem, but not with each other. The root of their problem was to be discovered deep within their lives. Although they were very much in love, for their love to fully blossom, the roadblocks in their individual lives that had been constructed over many years had to be dismantled. As that very painful and costly process would take place, a new beginning would emerge whereby God would have His rightful place in their hearts, and that being the case, their lives would be rebuilt on a solid foundation and their stories would be very different.

We welcome you into our journey through a maze filled with unrealistic expectations, fears, the need to be needed, living under the false premise of pleasing others at any expense, and the utter devastation that would bring these false beliefs to a crashing halt! God in His mercy saw fit to redeem our characters as His grace, love, peace, and kindness replaced our human striving that used to compel us. We both tried so hard to serve Him but lost something along the way—that something was the joy of the Lord.

As God's beautiful Spirit was allowed to replace the false beliefs that were in place for many years, the process of healing—though most painful—was begun in the life of our characters. Our two hearts would be melted, mended, and knit together by the compelling grace and compassion of our Lord. We now invite you to come on in and take a look at two lives, transformed by the power of their awesome God. You are most welcome into our hearts. But be warned, God may speak to you through our story! Are you ready?

As you read this story, please be aware that at times Bob is sharing his thoughts, and then Joan will share her thoughts to give you the perspective of the man and the woman and how we each affect one another or are affected by situations differently. It is our desire that we clearly share how important it is to be honest with each other, ourselves, and with God so our hearts may be free to experience all of life.

It is our prayer for you that you will be encouraged along your journey through this life with God's love and direction. Open your heart to see the bigger picture. He has so much in store for each of us if we will take Him at His Word and follow His leading.

Enjoy your adventure with God!

Bob and Joan Galasso

Chapter 1

An Invitation

The date was March 6, 2002. It was early on a Wednesday morning that started out like any other day. Before the rising of the sun that morning, I checked our e-mail as usual. While looking over the current mail, I came across an e-mail address that I had not seen, and my curiosity caused me to click that address first. Upon reading the letter, tears of joy streamed down my face as my heart was filled with the goodness of God. Had not this letter been the beginning of a vision for a new ministry that God put on my heart the previous summer? I called out to my wife, "Joanie come quickly, you have got to read this!" At that moment in time, there was silence as both of us looked at each other and wept with tears of joy, she said, "That's it! We will pray about this, and I know the answer is yes!" I said, "Yes, this is what we have been waiting for God to open up for us in ministry. We did not know where we would go or to whom." We stopped immediately and prayed, as His peace regarding our decision was clearly evident to both of us. We would say yes and trust God for His provision to honor the following request:

> Date: 3/6/2002 5:43 am   Eastern Standard Time
>
> Dear Bob and Joan, Greetings from Taiwan!
>
> Spring already is in the air here, reminding us again of God's renewing work in our lives. Today I received an email from Mike Sohm that you are interested in becoming a Pastoral Care Team for one of our C&MA (The Christian & Missionary Alliance) fields, and that you want to make yourselves available to speak at a Field Forum or a Prayer Retreat.
> Please sit down before reading the next paragraph.
> Would you be available to speak this year at our Field Forum? The dates are June 24-30, 2002.
> I realize that there is not much time left before this year's Field Forum. I also realize that this June date may not fit your schedule under such short notice. Our situation is that two weeks ago, the speaker that our Taiwan field had lined up for this year's Field Forum had to back out. The other potential speakers that I communicated with during these two weeks have not been able to re-arrange their schedules to come. Despite this, I am certain that the Lord is preparing His special servant for this important ministry. I am writing this e-mail to see if you are these "special servants of the Lord" for us.
> If you are available and willing, I would like to formally extend this invitation to you on behalf of the Field Leadership Team and the missionaries of the C&MA's Taiwan Field. We would be delighted if both of you could come. If you wish, we would provide opportunities for both of you to minister to us.
> ... We realize that you may need some time to pray about this, but we would appreciate hearing from you at your earliest convenience, especially as we now are only a few months away from Field Forum. We will be praying for

the Lord to direct and guide you as you consider this invitation. Our field presently is going through challenging transitions, and we are certain that God has something special in store both for our speaker and us.
I look forward to hearing from you soon.

Cordially in Christ,
Doyle Carlblom
Field Director, Taiwan Field

As we read this letter, my mind went back to a time about six months prior to this invitation when I sensed the Holy Spirit was preparing us for a ministry overseas. At that time, I shared with Joanie that I believed that something special would be opening up in June 2002. Not knowing at that time where we would go or to whom we might minister, we prayed and trusted God for His leading for the coming days. When I read the June dates, my heart leaped for joy as God's presence with us that morning was very real and He would bring to pass what He was preparing us for in His time. We replied immediately with a joyful yes! We also at that moment prayed specifically asking God to provide the finances for such a trip. Not knowing at that time what the cost of the trip would be, we committed our need into God's capable Hands and trusted Him for the funds that would be needed. We found out later that the cost for such a trip would be about $3,000. We began to ask God for $ 3,000 and trusted that since He was the One who was calling us, He would also be the One to provide for us in ways of His choosing. We were delighted to see His marvelous provision as the funds were there when the tickets needed to be purchased. The total amount of funds that were allocated for this ministry trip was $3,025. We rejoiced at God's provision and continued to prepare for this ministry opportunity. This would be the beginning of a new walk of faith unlike any other Joanie and I had previously experienced. We both knew we would wait on God from that moment on in new ways for the days to come.

As I read this e-mail with Bobby, I knew my answer was, "Yes, I will come to your Field Forum." At the same time, I found myself saying, "How can I do this, Lord? Go to missionaries? What could I possibly tell them that they don't already know? What could I say that would be of interest to them?" Although these questions bombarded my mind, I knew God wanted my husband and me to go.

In my heart of hearts, I loved missions and every time we got a chance to go to General Council (the annual conference of The Christian & Missionary Alliance), I cheered inside during the missionaries' parade as they all marched in the clothes of their country and carried their flags. I wondered why God had never called me to be among these great people. Now, here was this marvelous invitation staring at me from the computer. Would I come to Taiwan to minister to the missionaries? Yes, I will. Thank You, Lord that You would use me to bring encouragement to these special servants of yours.

---*

This transition into a new ministry calling actually began several years ago as God was molding us both through many experiences that would prepare us for such a ministry.

---

*This symbol denotes that Joan is expressing her point of view.

To fully appreciate our leap of faith, we must take you back several years in our ministry experience. Those years were filled with much frustration and noise in our lives as we had a philosophy that the best way to approach ministry would be by working harder.

Chapter 2
Working Harder

Have you ever heard the phrase, "working hard or hardly working"? Well, the first part of that question was certainly the way I lived as far back as I can remember. Although to work hard is quite honorable and most accepted in our culture, to be driven to live for work is quite another story. A large part of the way we function, I believe, can be traced back to the choices we make regarding what role models we follow. It also helps to understand the primary reason we made those choices. How could a young man who grew up with a solid background where God was taught, honored, loved, and worshipped get caught up in working so hard for the Lord that he lost sight of the joy of the Lord?

I bought into the philosophy of those who were older than me in ministry who painted the following picture, and along the way I did not see where this was taking me. While in my early twenties, I listened to those more seasoned than I speak of how hard they served our Lord. There was, of course, no time for vacations, not much room for family, and a day off would be considered a luxury. I thought if those in ministry for three to four decades before me did it that way, certainly it was a goal I would strive to reach. That was my problem! For the next fifteen years, I strove. I did not take the time to interview these spiritually driven servants regarding their family lives, their health, balance in their lives, or their true intimacy with God Himself. After all, if ministries are growing, people like what they see. All things being equal, they were doing at least as well as others in ministry. What else mattered?

If ministry alone is all that matters, then our entire framework of thinking will filter through that ministry funnel, regardless of what's lacking in other important facets of our lives. How could I have gotten so far away from living out the grace of God? How could I have replaced that wonderful opportunity with such unrealistic standards? How could I have accepted living under serious stress as a normal way of life?

Part of my problem during those most hectic years was I had developed goals around pleasing the wrong audience for the wrong reason. As I would work harder at getting people to like me, I did not realize I was gradually losing touch with the person I really was. I did not even care enough to find out as long as I stayed busy. Looking back, I realize now that I was setting myself up for a hard crash later as I heaped more work on myself, not out of necessity, but out of my driven desire to become all things to all people at any cost. Well, there certainly is a cost and guess who eventually pays the price?

In my case my immediate family paid the greatest price. My wife, Joan, and our three children during those early years of ministry had a father and a husband who was like a revolving door just passing through in his own home. Although I can remember having good intentions, I often allowed the emergencies of others to take priority during many family evenings. I wish I knew then what I know now about placing voluntary boundaries around one's life that provide stability and balance. I remember several times flying out the door to do really important things, believing those I loved would surely understand. Throughout those many years, I failed to ask my family how they felt about this disappearing dad and husband. What did they think about this super busy man, and what impact did these repeated actions have on their lives? At times, I may have interpreted the silence of my family regarding my busyness as their agreement that this way of living was not only fine but also the way it should be. After all, we must keep on keeping on.

Now with hindsight, I have come to realize that their silence really meant they didn't want to rock the boat, when in fact, the boat desperately needed to be capsized! How much better it would have been to realize we needed to have a mid-course correction than to continue to go downhill without even knowing it! I am certain though, that at that time in my life I would not have heard them. How do I know that? There were times when Joanie would say to me, "Bobby, we need to change the way we do things." My response was, "This is the way you do ministry." What an answer from a worn-out man who was doing it the wrong way and did not even know it. However, when you believe what you are doing is right, it is right for you. Here was yet another false belief that would soon prove to come tumbling down as I realized that working harder was not working.

It is interesting to note that about this time in my life I recorded many thoughts in my personal diary. I read of others who in their journey realized that the work of the Lord could actually be a temptation to take us away from our communion with God. My strength was being eroded day by day by doing good things for God while missing the most important thing. As I traveled, preached and counseled, it was my fellowship with God that was most needed in my life. And yet in my desire to please God, I had lost sight of the blessed truth that it was my heart that He was after and not my work for Him. As I look back on those days, it seems I was reading and writing things I needed to know, and even agreed with, while at the same time missing the boat as far as my own personal application. I wonder, how many of us have lived the same way at some time in our lives. Oh to have realized back then that, for God's people, worship must come before work.

Even while serving as pastor during those days, I wonder how much worship really happened. My focus would be on the preaching about to follow, how many were in the service that morning, who was not there, and on and on. I know none of you have ever struggled with this sort of thing, but I have and can remember how those times would rob me of my own intimacy with the Father. I am now realizing in my journey with God that He truly does speak to me when I am still and seeking Him above His work. Although the things He does for me are great, He is preparing me afresh day by day for ministry as I find my entire satisfaction in Him alone. Wow! To focus on God Himself, not what He does, but who He is. It thrills my heart!

During my busiest days filled with turmoil, disappointments, and never having enough time (what a false belief that is), there was then and still is now a wonderful truth about the character of God that I would like to leave with you before Joanie continues this part of our journey. It is found in Isaiah 49:13-16:

> Shout for joy, O heavens; rejoice, O earth; burst into song, O mountains! For the Lord comforts his people and will

have compassion on his afflicted ones. But Zion said, 'The Lord has forsaken me, the Lord has forgotten me.' Can a mother forget the baby at her breast and have no compassion on the child she has borne? Though she may forget, I will never forget you! See, I have engraved you on the palms of my hands; your walls are ever before me."

I hung on to what I did know about God, while everything else around me was about to come crumbling down.

As the pastor's wife, I entered wholeheartedly into ministry right beside my husband—together we would burn out for Jesus. After all, isn't that what a committed Christian does? A godly person holds back nothing—gives everything to honor and serve God. Whatever it took to be in ministry, I was prepared to do it. So, whenever my husband's heart was stirred by God to move to another church, I would have to deal with packing up my house and uprooting my children. In the beginning days when the children were small, that wasn't too hard, but as they got older and were more aware of leaving their friends and their house, it became very difficult. As their mother, my heart would be very torn between my children's need to remain with their school and neighborhood friendships and my husband's call to minister to another church. I really didn't think moving bothered me when it came right down to it. I was only concerned about my husband obeying the call of God and my children being content. I was not wise in overlooking my own heart in this area. My needs were as important as any member of my family, but I did not look at it this way. I ignored myself and gave my attention to making sure everyone else got through the transition and to packing up the old house and unpacking the new house. At first, moving was exciting, and I tried to view it as an adventure. Very quickly, though, moving turned to upheaval and hardship on the family unit.

One morning after we had moved, I was making up the bed when I broke down and wept. I didn't want to move from our last ministry. I loved my home. My children loved their school and were happy with their friends. I wanted to live there forever. I had never before allowed my feelings to surface, and that morning my feelings came out in tears coursing down my face. I was alone, so I just dried my tears and kept my feelings to myself. I didn't want to upset my husband or cause him to think I didn't want to be in my new home and church. I tried once again to tell myself that I did this for God, and He would take care of me. Now I know I could easily have shared my feelings with my husband. Together we could have talked about the change, the move, and the normal effects moving has on a family, but I didn't understand about feelings back then. I thought feelings would spoil everything and that covering them up or asking God to forgive me was the best way to handle them. This thinking is not true and only caused my feelings to go deeper inside myself and emerge in hurtful ways. The truth is feelings are alive, they are a part of us, and they will remain in us and cause problems until they are finally allowed expression.

So you can see, as a young woman who wanted to please God, I would never interfere with my husband's calling to serve. I would put myself aside completely and let him go anywhere, do anything at anytime to serve God and the church. This is how I viewed myself as the wife of a pastor.

Working Harder

It would be a long time before I realized how important it is to take care of my heart and myself.

For several years, I believed ministry meant serving the needs of others without regard to my own needs. In my mind, this was a given fact of ministry. For a long time, I never questioned how we were living. When our children came along and our family was young, it became increasingly difficult to maintain this self-imposed lifestyle of burning out for God. I found myself having to work harder at being happy whenever the phone rang and someone needed the pastor. One evening something unexpected happened to make me realize what an awful effect this was having on my heart for my family and the church.

We had been in ministry for about ten years now, and our path had a huge "detour ahead" sign on it. On this particular night, we planned to have a special evening together. I was so happy as I set the table for dinner. We were going to have a wonderful meal and then a wonderful evening of just being together as a family. In the middle of placing the food on the table, the phone rang. I already knew as Bobby hung up that he had to leave—an emergency—someone needed something. I smiled and said it was OK and made sure he left with only his need of ministry on his mind. As soon as the door closed behind him, I lashed out with anger and resentment at the empty room. It wasn't all right, and I hated that he had to leave for the hundredth time!

Instead of seeing this as a normal, human reaction when you feel ripped off at the last minute, I viewed my reaction as sinful and displeasing to God. I cried bitterly, asking God for forgiveness and trying desperately to hold on to my belief that my husband had to go—he was a pastor and together we had to lay down our all to serve God. Only it wasn't working for me anymore. My view of serving God was falling apart, and the necessary detour was just ahead.

I, (Bob), would imagine that by now in our story, you are beginning to see where we might be headed. Regardless of how hard we worked, how many new ideas we tried, or how dedicated we were, this way of life and ministry was *not working*! Both our lives were by now filled with several false beliefs that we were living under that were burying us, and we did not know it. We kept thinking all this hard work would pay off eventually. So where was the grace of God throughout this entire human endeavor?

Well, His Grace was there all the time, but our efforts and striving were so compelling that we missed what He was attempting to do along the way. We were too busy serving Him to see it.

All of this human effort would soon prove to show itself for what it really was. You guessed it! Human effort! That is why it was all destined to fall apart sooner or later. As things continued to get busier and working harder at this ministry effort became the norm, I had a sense about me that things were not going well. The machinery was moving, but on the inside, the body and mind were beginning to rebel. My inner man was screaming for attention and peace, but my driven nature would not listen and continued to feed the false beliefs I was by now totally sold out to. What were they? Please people at any cost. Be all things to all people all of the time. Never say no or someone may not like you. Stay busy, look busy, and be sure those around you understood how hard you were working. Have as many people in your home as possible in the shortest time possible in order to know them sooner. Wow! That wears me out just writing this, but that was the way I was living.

As you might imagine, this way of living could not continue forever without a major price being paid along the way. There must be a better way to be a pastor, husband, and father. The problem was that I had done the best I could, and yet my plan was failing. So if my plan was not working, even though I was working the plan, what went wrong?

Chapter 3
What Went Wrong?

After fifteen years of hard work attending seminars, adding more hours, trying to please more people, and staying extremely busy, I had lost my identity as a person and was living continuously in the role of a pastor. I was slowly, through the process of time, losing touch with who I was as I was consumed with what I did. I would preach about the peace of God and yet not be still enough in my own heart to know this wonderful peace for myself.

It is a terrible thing to be living in your home but not really be there in your head. Everything at this stage in my life was related to work. I can remember a day when one of my children was speaking to me, and I was, as usual, tuned out. While he continued to talk to me, he placed his hands under my face and turned my head back toward him while saying, "Dad, I am talking to you. Look at me."

In that moment, I realized I was drifting away during many conversations. I was missing what was going on at the time, not living in the moment but in the future—always planning, always preparing, always considering what the next thing would be on my to do list. Yet it never all got done.

Surely the harder I worked, the more God would approve of me. What a lie! Where did that come from, and why was I sucked into such a false belief? As I look back on those years, I believe a large part of the reason for my living in those false beliefs was that I really did not accept the truth that God Himself loved me and accepted me regardless of my performance, results, or status.

So what went wrong? Just about everything! Things had gotten so bad at this point that whatever it took to look and stay busy, I would do. The illustration I am about to share may cause you to shake your head and say to yourself, "This man really had a problem!" You are right! I really did! As this story develops, you will see the Hand of God transforming my life for His Glory in His Time.

The following story is true, and the names *have not* been changed to protect the innocent. I, being the key character in this story, have given myself permission to tell the truth.

It was late one afternoon, and I had returned home from work. I had already worked about nine or ten hours, when just before dinnertime, the phone rang. Someone wanted to come over to talk for a while. Now most normal folks would have said, "Now is not a good time," or "Come on over for a few minutes." Not me! You see, I needed to be needed, and in the process I would demonstrate how busy I was while I fit you in to my schedule.

So, with this false belief, I proceeded to get out of my chair and do what I believed was necessary to show the person coming over that I was very busy. What I am about to tell you is simply an indicator of how bad things had gotten by this point. I quickly went to our large dining room table that had nothing on it and placed the following items. I gathered together a couple Bibles, a few commentaries, a notebook, a few other books, and a pen. Then I opened these books and spread them out like I normally did while studying on the entire surface of the table. I waited for the doorbell to ring, and when it did, I sat down with pen in hand, books open, looking deep in thought, and said, "Come in." Mission accomplished! The person came in and saw how busy I was. We spoke for a while, and then he (or she) left.

Now that I had looked busy, I collected all the books, Bibles, notebooks, and pens and put everything away to get ready for dinner. Wow! Sounds pretty weird, doesn't it? It was, and I did not even know at the time that I had a problem because this type of obsessive behavior had become the norm in my life. You see, whatever it took to give the appearance of being a busy pastor, I would provide free of charge. Now there is absolutely no blame being directed elsewhere as I have owned this behavior as a result of my acceptance of the false belief of needing the approval of others.

The colors of life begin to fade, and the beauty of sunrises and sunsets lose their radiance to the one who takes his eyes off his Creator and places them on mere men. The twinkle is lost in the eye, the smile vanishes from the face and the joy of the heart escapes the one whose focus has shifted from God to man. That shifting focus would lead this struggling man back to a desperate cry for help to his God. And do you know what? God met this man in a glorious way. A little later in this book I will share that story.

During our ministry in one community, I remember starting my day at 8:30 in the morning and having one or two weekly appointments before I got to the church. I was working three or four nights a week and had three nights a week with my family. As the years progressed, I started my day earlier and earlier until I was starting work at 6:30

in the morning, with a regular weekly appointment before that time. I was not compensating for the additional time later in the day. As a matter of fact, after a few years, I was then working six days and six nights. The ministry did not demand this of me. My compulsion to do more and work harder led me to this schedule.

During these days, we were having people over to our home about twice a week for dinner, *Every week!* Although I asked Joanie if this regular schedule of having so many people over for dinner was all right with her, I could tell it was not her thing. She said, "I don't really know how to do this, but it is OK." I really did not believe it was OK, but being driven, I continued to invite as many to our home as would consent to come, and we kept this pace for years. I was sensing this was not working out too well after a while, but we did not discuss it; after all, we were reaching out to those who needed us. I wonder whose needs were *really* being met?

Once again, I did not speak up and let my husband know my real feelings. I did not grow up in a home that had people over for dinner and fellowship like my husband's family did. He was accustomed to having large groups of people around, but it frustrated me. I would struggle inside my mind, "I can't do this. It makes me so nervous to have people in my home. I don't like the pressure it puts on me to get dinner ready for them and my children."

I only breathed a sigh of relief when we were able to sit down to the table and conversation would begin. I knew I could be quiet to gather my nerves. My husband would carry the conversation, and I could sit back and just make sure the children behaved. I realize now that God overcame my weaknesses even without my realizing it at the time. How much better it would have been had I been honest and said what I thought about all these invitations. I would then have been free to enjoy the people and relax and be myself without the stress of performing. I would have been a part of making the decision to ask our visitors and that would have enabled me to have an open heart and relaxed mind during their visits.

Discussing the difficulties I experienced making dinner after a Sunday morning church schedule or sharing my desire to simply be alone with my family would have allowed my heart to feel cared for. I wouldn't have felt put out or that this was something my husband demanded I make the best of. What a difference when you can enjoy something because it is what you want to do as well as what your husband wants. I was being dishonest with God, my guests, and my husband!

I may not be able to do that part of my life over again, but I can sure make the most of my present situation. Sharing my thoughts and feelings about important decisions has greatly improved our relationship. In this case as in all cases before our Lord Jesus, honesty is the best policy.

I, (Bob), can remember one morning, after working about five hours, when I came home for a moment, on my way to somewhere else. No one was home, and as I was about to be on my way, the phone rang. I answered it by saying, "Hello" and the voice on the other end said, "Pastor Bob, what are you doing home?" Now, allow me to step out of this story for a moment to ask a question. Might the normal response to such a question be, "Can I help you?" Or, 'I just got in, can I take a message?" Neither of these were my response. You see, it was 11:30 in the morning, and I believed (there goes that false belief system again), that I had no right to be home at that time or at least I needed to give my reasons for being there. My response was, "Oh, I am just passing through. I started work at 6:30 this morning, had some appointments, happened to be in the area, and I am soon going out the door to visit someone with a full day ahead of me." Wow! What a load to dump on that caller! At this juncture in ministry, I had advanced from working fifty-five hours a week to an average of seventy hours a week. My mind was always racing. I would lie in bed at night needing an hour or more to fall asleep, as I was already thinking about tomorrow or the events of the past day. I often asked myself, "Is there a better way to do ministry?" I would say to Joanie, "I am not doing well." But we did not know what to do to get out of this routine that was destined to cause our lives to come to a crashing halt. What used to be ministry flowing out of joy was becoming a life of obligation and doing what was necessary for survival.

While writing this chapter, I came across a truth that when realized, puts this issue of human striving in its proper perspective. Andrew Murray wrote:

> When the pressure of work for Christ is allowed to be the excuse for our not finding time to seek and secure His own presence and power in it as our chief need, our sense of absolute dependence on God is not right.[1]

During those days of my human striving while things were not working, I was still engaged in a regular time with my Lord through prayer and reading His Word. So what was the problem? You see, when we try to mix a little God and a little of ourselves we are bound to come up with a lack of change and depth on the inside. The outward appearance in my case was looking as if things were fine, but inwardly there was a great hole deep within my soul that could never be satisfied with anything outside of an intimate relationship with my Lord.

I can remember even going through the motions of Bible reading and prayer, while still trying to help God out by working for Him. As long as I continued to believe I was doing a work for Him, I worked relentlessly to accomplish the goal of attempting to please God through my service and please people at the same time. This way of life and ministry would soon prove to be another false belief that was not working.

During the summer of 1987, I wrote the following observations in my diary:

> But He knows the way that I take; when He has tested me, I will come forth as gold (Job 23:10). God wants His children to trust Him even when they cannot understand Him. When God is going to do something wonderful, He'll often begin with a difficulty.

There is some good news in the middle of all of this striving. God is there for those who really desire Him. "But if from there you seek the Lord your God, you will find him if you look for him with all your heart and with all your soul" (Deuteronomy 4:29). There are times in this life when we are strung out so tight, so involved and overcommitted, so focused and intense that we desperately need to back off and take a break.

As I wrote this chapter, I came across some good food for thought regarding an illustration that is most appropriate to the issue of needing rest from ongoing stress. This illustration is taken from a reading out of *The Daily Bread* publication:

> According to tradition, when the Apostle John was overseer in Ephesus, his hobby was raising pigeons. It is said that on one occasion another elder passed his house as he returned from hunting and saw John playing with one of his birds. The man gently chided him for spending his time so frivolously. John looked at the hunter's bow and remarked that the string was loose. "Yes," said the elder, "I always loosen the string of my bow when it's not in use. If it stayed tight, it would lose its resilience and fail me in the hunt." John responded, "And I am now relaxing the bow of my mind so that I may be better able to shoot the arrows of divine truth."[2]

What a great example of our regular need to back off at times from our own self-imposed stresses and tyranny of the urgent. There is a great example that Jesus Himself modeled for us of this great need during His public ministry. In the Gospel of Mark we read an account of Jesus' response to a stressful situation recorded for us in Mark 6: 30-32:

> The apostles gathered around Jesus and reported to him all that they had done and taught. Then, because so many people were coming and going that they did not even have a chance to eat, he said to them, 'Come with me by yourselves to a quiet place and get some rest.' So they went away by themselves in a boat to a solitary place.

During those busy days in my life, I would have had more balance had I made that practice of retreating to a quiet, solitary place a regular part of my life. God, however, would take all my shortcomings and, in the years to follow, put within my heart a desire and a plan that would provide peace and restoration for this weary man.

As I look at what my husband has been writing, I am reminded of those years when work and schedules consumed us. At the time, I did not realize what was going wrong. The working-harder mentality is not only draining on the husband, it is also hard on the wife and his children. On many of our family vacations it would take several days before he would really join us. He was there physically, but not mentally. We'd be walking the beach and his conversation would be about the job or planning for the next vacation. I would complain inside myself, *If I have to listen to him plan our next vacation before we have even enjoyed this one, I'll scream,* or *If I have to listen to one more thing about his job and his concerns that things are all right while he is gone . . . I just don't want to hear it anymore.* Finally after a few days, I could relax and exhale with relief that his conversations had changed and he was at last truly on his vacation with his family. I did not speak my mind to him and, as always, listened as best I could.

I know now that working harder is not God's way. It removed our husband and father from his home, and the children and I were left with a void that only his presence could fill. I have learned that speaking up and telling my husband how I feel about what he is doing is the best thing I could do. Many times a change in direction can happen that is beneficial to the family when honest feelings are shared.

I am thankful to God for causing my heart to share my thoughts and feelings about what happens in our lives. God can direct and use honesty between a husband and wife. There is nothing to fear in an atmosphere of love and acceptance, and I had to learn that. Perhaps if I had spoken up about how I felt concerning Bobby's work-a-holic tendencies, we wouldn't have had to go through such difficult experiences. This is something I will never know, but I can thank God for using these difficulties and holding us while we learned the lessons He had for us. He is a loving God, and as His children we can be sure He will work all things together for our good and His glory. Using work to satisfy a drive within us is harmful and wrong. God used this to bring us to the end of ourselves and back to a position where He could use us and show us a better way.

I was coming to grips with the fact that we needed a change and we needed it right away. I didn't know if my husband would buy into my suggestion that we needed to slow down. We discussed specific ways to accomplish this, like taking regular days off, going on a trip and cutting back hours. When he agreed to these changes, I was delighted. However, we would soon come to realize that in fact, it would be too little, too late.

Chapter 4
Too Little Too Late

As both of us were now beginning to understand we were in a situation that needed to change, we had tossed around ideas to fix our problem. The term "too little to late" would serve us well at this time in our journey since we both recognized that an immediate change was necessary for survival.

I use the word *survival* because that had become the mindset we were in during those dark days. I remember Joanie saying to me at that time, "We need some time away." Of course by then we needed more than that, but we thought it might be a good beginning. We also discussed slowing down the pace of both ministry and our personal lives. Surely we could re-evaluate our priorities and find solutions.

This was not to be the case. Fifteen years of unrealistic expectations, lack of sleep, a hurried pace, and being stuck on the treadmill of working harder would prove to be too much for this tired pastor. During this chapter of our journey, Joanie and I were making plans to get away just about anywhere and the sooner the better. However, there was no place I could go to escape from myself. My driven desire to do more and the pain I was carrying was now becoming more than either of us could bear.

For those of you who are reading this and thinking to yourselves, *That was really a weak man,* you are certainly correct. I could identify with the Apostle Paul who after he had petitioned the Lord to take away his thorn in the flesh, was told by the Lord:

> My grace is sufficient for you. For my power is made perfect in weakness. Therefore I will boast all the more gladly about my weaknesses, so that Christ's power may rest on me. That is why, for Christ's sake, I delight in weaknesses, in insults, in hardships, in persecutions, in difficulties. For when I am weak, then I am strong.
> (2 Corinthians 12:9-10)

Was I a candidate for that condition? You bet I was! By now I was about as low as a person could get. My mind was no longer focused. My fears grew greater. My future looked darker. Hope? What was that? And yet, God was there. I was not any good for any one, but He did not abandon me.

Let me say at this point, dear reader, that we need to be very careful when we say to God, "Do whatever it takes, Lord!" That is a serious request! I wrote the following heart cry to my Lord May 12, 1988:

> Jesus, in the light of your soon return may every day of my life count for eternity! More souls must come to you before it is too late! BREAK ME UP AND POUR YOUR PRECIOUS SPIRIT THROUGH ME! WHATEVER IT TAKES!

Wow! I would come to realize in the months to follow the need to abandon myself to God alone and place myself back on the potter's wheel. Soon I would be falling apart. I would need to *know* the truth of Scripture and the faithfulness of my God when *nothing else* mattered or could be understood, either by myself or those around this soon-to be shell of a man. I wrote these words found in Jeremiah 17:7-8:

> But blessed is the man who trusts in the Lord, whose confidence is in him. He will be like a tree planted by the water that sends out its roots by the stream. It does not fear when heat comes; its leaves are always green. It has no worries in a year of drought and never fails to bear fruit.

As I read through and meditated on the following Scripture, little did I realize then what the full impact of those words would have on my about-to-be-broken life. In fact these words would change me forever. Jeremiah 18:6 states, " 'O house of Israel, can I not do with you as this potter does?' declares the Lord. 'Like clay in the hand of the potter, so are you in my hand, O house of Israel.' " My one consolation during those days was that my future was not in my own hands (praise God), the hands of the church, the hands of any human help, but I was in His Hands that would prove to be large enough and strong enough to not only carry me but set my feet on His solid foundation once again.

Just a few months before my total breakdown of mind, body, and spirit, I was seeing the need for slowing down and a quieter way of life. I always had a lot to say to God, but what about listening? I used to bring Him my talents, my experience, my ideas, but now I soon would be presenting

Him with my failures, broken dreams, anger, frustration, and shattered life. Toward the end of May, 1988, I was writing to God what I thought I needed, but my way of life, thinking, and ministry up to that point had finally taken its toll. I wrote, "Lord, may I spend more time in 'silence' before you!"

There is a great temptation in prayer to talk to God without being still to allow Him to talk to us. As I find myself presenting to God my emptiness rather than plans or solutions, it is at that very time that He provides the wisdom, counsel and direction that I could never have produced on my own. My Father fills my empty hands with the freshness of His creativity, love, and inspiration.

These hands that had been full of so much human effort would soon be empty. This road would ultimately lead to freedom, but there were still some days, weeks, months, and years ahead of me at the Potter's Wheel for which I am eternally grateful to God.

I am learning along the way that, as long as we have the grace of God, failure is not final. If there were ever a time in my life when I would spell *Failure* with a capital F, the days to follow would become in my eyes a great failure. However, my gracious Heavenly Father does not see these failures as final. He knows my end from my beginning (Psalm 139) and allows whatever will happen in my life to make me more like Himself. I came to realize during those long days and nights that God does not shield us from life's storms; He shelters us in life's storms.

During the writing of this book, I had a thought that I believe is true. It typified where I was during the time in my life that I just described to you. It is not a quote from someone else (that I know of), so feel free to use it if you like. I recently came to understand that it is difficult to fix your problem when you are in the problem, and then you find out you are the problem. You see, I used to be a fixer of others (not really, but another false belief. Are you counting all these false beliefs that I used to live under? Do any of them sound familiar?), but when you cannot see the forest for the trees yourself, you are in desperate need of help. Although I did not know where to go or what to say, God was in control and used all of my detours to bring me out of this deep dark hole and eventually into His glorious light!

I found myself wanting desperately to be isolated, away from all people and situations (not exactly in the job description of a pastor, husband, or a father). I would not answer the phone, go to the door, or want to be with people at this point in my downward spiral.

Here is an example of how bad things had become. This occurred in the afternoon of what would turn out to be the darkest night of my life. It was a Friday afternoon in October 1988. Joanie had called me at the church and asked if I could meet her and our children at a local McDonald's for lunch. We agreed on a time, and as I pulled up to the restaurant, a very dark cloud of despair and anger came over me. I did not want to be with the people who meant the world to me, my family.

We met, went inside, and ordered our food. When the food came, we sat at a table. A child behind where we were sitting began to scream, and all of a sudden I lost it! Every time the child behind me cried, I became more tense and irritable. A few seconds later, I got out of my seat and went to a table by myself. My family followed behind, looking horrified and wondering what was going on. Joanie tried once again to explain my behavior to our children who just wanted to have lunch with their dad. I did not look up and stormed out of the restaurant! These dark moods had become more frequent, longer lasting, and more intense. I knew at this point I needed help but had no idea what to do.

At this point, my husband was in trouble, and I was at a loss for what to do. We were like a train speeding down the track, totally out of control, headed to crash. I wanted to get us off before that happened. *We have to get away!* I'd think. I can remember the anxious feelings rising up from my heart and filling my mind with fear. *What is going to happen to him if he doesn't get away?* I felt so boxed in. To every suggestion I made, he had an objection concerning the church. "Who will preach for me? It isn't that easy to get someone, you know," he would inform me. He wouldn't cooperate with me, and I could feel the crash coming. I was desperate...

Usually Bobby is an energetic person who enjoys people. So when he started withdrawing into himself, I started worrying. My reaction was to try to make him happy and explain his behavior to the children. "Daddy's just tired," I would tell them. "He will be fine."

These dark moods weren't like him, and it made me uncomfortable. I remember one time as he lay in his bed with the lights out, I told him about Isaiah 40:31, "But those who hope in the Lord will renew their strength, they will soar on wings like eagles; they will run and not grow weary, they will walk and not faint." Therefore, we must be doing something wrong because we were weary and fainting. Our way of ministering was not like Isaiah at all. We were running out of steam.

I was not able to get us off the doomed train and avert the course of our direction. God was in control now, and He was preserving us by the Holy Spirit and His awesome hand of protection while we could not care for ourselves. He had a plan, and He used our misconceptions to bring us to the end of ourselves. Only He could redeem our brokenness and make sense of our messes. He loves us that much.

God caused Jeremiah 29:11-13 to come alive in the lives of His children as He brought life and healing to our pain and losses. His desire was for restoration and to fill our lives with hope and promise. God's plans and purposes for Bobby and me involved our falling apart. It was the only way He could get our attention and make the necessary corrections to our very needy lives. We were about to be rebuilt from the ground floor up, and although it was painful, it would be done within the loving hands of our Father God.

I believe that is why James 1:2-5 tells us not to run from our trials but to embrace them. It is in the depths of our despair and pain that we hear God if we listen. He is there in the midst of our brokenness. And He is there when we feel the huge sense of loss that is so large we can hardly breathe. When we allowed this trial to have its perfect work in our hearts and to affect our lives through this awful testing, we were forever changed. We were transformed by the renewing of our minds as Romans 12:1-2 tells us.

God's Word is powerful and sharper than any two-edged sword. As Hebrews 4:12 says, it penetrates to the soul and spirit, joints and marrow; and it judges the thoughts and attitudes of the heart. And His Word was meant to be lived in our lives not just studied in our minds.

God wants us to experience Him in every sense of the word. His life is our healing. His word is our mainstay. He will see us through our darkest hour. It is His job to show Himself faithful. Scripture is full of His stories directing us to see His glory and that He is who He says He is—our God, strong and mighty.

His Word is our life. That is why He told us that heaven and earth may pass away, but His Word will never pass away. He can be counted on. When we rest in Him—and get out of the way—then He can do His marvelous work in us that all our figuring out could never accomplish, but would only keep us lacking. We must let go and believe in Him, allowing Him to have our hearts and trusting Him with our lives, our children, and those closest to us.

He will never fail us and will always show us His unending love. The things He may do in our lives may cause us great hurt and to have questions, but we must persevere to be made mature and complete, not lacking in anything. God never intends to hurt us and leave us. He has a purpose and a plan, and we must use our strong will and place ourselves in His powerful hand. God is then able to do above and beyond what we could ask or think.

I believe our lives began to improve when we allowed God to have His rightful place, and we followed His plan instead of our own. God is so good to use all that we go through for His glory and our ultimate good. I love this awesome God with all my heart and my entire mind and all my strength.

Although I now know the observations I have just described for you to be true, something had to occur for us both to walk in this new way. Little did we know that before these new changes would occur, we would fall apart at the seams.

Chapter 5
Coming Apart at the Seams

"This can't be happening to me!" That was the cry of my heart and what came out of my mouth. It was a sad and lonely October morning in the fall of 1988. That day would be the beginning of a change that would affect me for the rest of my life. That Saturday would be like no other that I had ever known. There I was, clutching on to my shower door with a pain and despair that I had never experienced before. I cried out to my God with a heart filled with fear and terror saying, "This can't be happening to me!" I was on my way to a private hospital for what I thought would be a few days of rest. I was admitted immediately as a man full of exhaustion. I did not realize at the time that this would be the beginning of a most painful but necessary process of honesty that would, in the economy of God's time, be used for His glory and my benefit. How did I get to this place in my life?

After being in the ministry for over fifteen years and only thirty-seven years young, I was stunned at the reality of the situation that I had now been forced to face. I was utterly exhausted, angry, bewildered, and had no desire to be around people. Not anyone! Had I not enjoyed being with people all my life? For the first time ever, I felt truly alone. *Does anyone understand me?* I'd think. *What is really going on?* After tearfully watching my wife, Joanie, and a dear friend leave me in my hospital room, there I was, all alone. But God was there all the time, and I would come to understand more than ever before, that He alone is my Provider and Healer.

Throughout the next several weeks, I would come to the awareness that a large portion of my life was spent in my own vain attempt to please people. Although I was serving God, as I then believed He called me to, I also had a concern for the following questions: What do those around me think? How are they accepting me? Am I keeping everyone happy? Wait a minute, Bob! Is it not Jesus Christ you are to serve, worship, and put your full trust in for every area of your life? This was a question I asked of myself that demanded an answer. To be absolutely honest with myself and my God, I had to admit that I was living for the approval of others. I was often shattered when that approval was not there. My precious Heavenly Father had finally gotten my attention.

As a young child, I had accepted Jesus Christ into my life and have known His forgiveness and love for many years. My life's verse from God's holy Word is found in 2 Corinthians 5:17 which states, "Therefore, if anyone is in Christ, he is a new creation; the old had gone, the new has come!" Could my God take this tired child of His and transform him afresh into the man that He would desire me to be? Could I be changed into His likeness and freed from the bondage that I had often previously placed on myself regarding man's opinion and approval of me? The thought of a new way of living unto God and no longer under man has so captured my heart that my hope for you is to be encouraged with the miracle that my God has done for me and my family. Think of it! God takes us just as we are and molds us just as He desires for His glory. What a blessed opportunity to be touched by the Master.

During those days, I could only read about two sentences at a time before my concentration would be gone. I held on tightly to the Scripture taken from Psalm 35:27: "The Lord be exalted, who delights in the well-being of his servant." I clung to that Scripture for the next couple years.

"Bob, who are you?" This question was asked of me by a caring social worker during my forty-two days in the hospital. I proceeded to tell her with great assurance that I was a *pastor*—including all my business and family concerns. I began throwing up one smokescreen after another. I did not want to answer the question for which I did not have the answer.

A stripping away of another layer of my life was about to begin. Would I welcome it? *No way!* Was it necessary? *Absolutely!*

My doctor said, "Bob, if you continue this pace, you may not see forty years of age." Could it be that God had spared me literally by stopping me before it was too late? Only He knows that answer, but I knew right then and there, that the time had come to live life in a new way that would change me for the better for the rest of my life.

My denial had finally come to an end during a group therapy session when a nineteen-year-old girl said to me, "When are you going to stop being a pastor and become a person?" I hated that statement. I got angry and resentful until I admitted that she was raising the very question that I needed to be confronted with that day. In time, I thanked her and began getting back to basics as I came to God just as I was and let Him love me over and over again.

About thirty days into my program, I came home to visit my family for the day on a pass from the hospital. Well, that day would be quite different than what I had anticipated. Now the focus of attention would be on Joanie. What I found in her condition (while I was still a patient myself) was not good. She was coming apart at the seams right before my eyes. How could I help her when I still was receiving help and not even living at home yet? We had three young children at home with their father removed from the scene and their mother extremely fragile. Now what?

I tried to carry on as best I could in this desert place. After I left Bobby in the hospital, I was numb. I really tried to tell myself, "This is his problem. I must be there for him. He needs me to be strong. I need to help the children; they don't understand. I need to help the church; they don't understand." What I didn't say out loud or even to myself was, "I need help, I don't understand." I tried to do what I always did—get busy. Only this time it wouldn't work.

In the days that followed, I slowly withdrew completely into myself. I felt alone and embarrassed. I didn't know how to reach out for help and tell people my fears. I began to pull away from everyone. I didn't want phone calls. I didn't want to see anyone. I couldn't deal with questions because I had no answers and my hurt was too great. I didn't go anywhere. A few people brought food, and it was great because I had no desire to cook. Actually, I couldn't do anything. Everything was an effort, and I really didn't have the desire to get a handle on my situation. I couldn't sleep, so I was tired and lacked energy due to a very heavy, grief-stricken heart.

I was not prepared for my reaction during these days. To say it was hard for me puts it mildly. I was not expecting this awful feeling of loss to engulf me. A feeling of loneliness overwhelmed me, and I was scared. I functioned in the day—performing daily tasks and being there for the children—in the beginning. But soon, everything became too much for me to deal with, especially at night. I was alone once the children were in bed. It was here, in the evenings, that I would really experience a feeling of deep aloneness, despair, and loss. It was awful. I remember telling myself during one of these times, "It is OK. He'll be back. Don't take it so hard. He didn't die." But I couldn't help myself. The feeling of loss and hopelessness wouldn't leave me. I cried from deep within myself. I slept little and stopped eating.

I know some may have tried to get close to me and find out what was wrong, but I wouldn't let them near me. At that point, I couldn't let people get near me. So I was caught between desiring people to come close and a feeling of embarrassment that caused me to push people away.

There was something else happening to me during Bobby's hospitalization. I was quickly and without knowing it becoming overwhelmed by depression. My whole outlook was clouded, and I couldn't think clearly because I was in such despair. My emotions were so sad I went numb and just performed the routines of life. It was in this state that I stopped going to church and seeing people.

This is also about the time my husband came home on one of his visits from the hospital. When he saw the shape I was in plus the fact that I was crying and telling him I couldn't be with the children anymore, he quickly made arrangements for me to come to the hospital with him, so they could examine me. It was decided that I should be hospitalized for clinical depression. Bobby called my mother to come and stay with the children who were confused and sad by what was going on with their parents.

    I didn't understand why I was in this hospital or what was the matter with me. I had so many questions. How was I to get better? What did I have to do? I let them admit me into the hospital. I signed my name agreeing to remain for three days in this locked unit. It ended up to be two weeks. I was moved to a different unit for four more weeks, and then I was released.

    During this hospitalization, I learned a little about depression. Depression is repressed anger or anger turned inward. I had to work on my feelings and let them out. It sounded strange to me. I wasn't used to expressing my feelings, and it took me a long time to own my anger. Nice people didn't get angry, so I worked hard at being a nice person. I viewed anger as sinful. I was a Christian—I didn't get angry.

    By the time I was released, I had connected with some of my feelings of anger. I learned that I had in fact stuffed my feelings and that expressing them would be the way to emotional health. When I came home, I tried to put my theories into practice, but it didn't work. After three months, I came apart at the seams again and had to be hospitalized a second time. This time I was experiencing an intense desire to end my life.

    It was in this state of mind that one night, while we were getting ready for bed, my husband asked, "Are you thinking about harming yourself?" I know that it was the Lord laying this on his mind because I never intended on telling him anything about the way I was feeling. After all, he was trying to return to the church and begin working on getting our lives back to normal. I didn't want to do anything to keep him from being a pastor again.

All my defenses were down and as I looked up at him, big tears fell down my face. This reaction was all he needed. From that time on, he wouldn't leave me alone. He and I decided to see my counselor and tell her what was going on.

I chose a Christian treatment center where I could deal with my suicidal thinking and try to get on the road to recovery. I didn't want anything to do with my family, the church, my parents—I just wanted to be left alone. I am glad now that my family did not leave me alone but at the time, I didn't care about anything.

As I went into the facility, I held on to only one thing— God loves me. I didn't want anyone talking to me about God or praying with me. In my heart, I knew that God would have to help me or I wasn't going to get well. I had tried one hospital, and I had learned a few important truths, but I needed more. This time it would be God or nothing.

I thank God with all my heart that He sustained me and caused me to live His promise, "I will never leave you, or forsake you," as I found healing during my stay at the treatment center. He kept me from ending my life and He enabled me to turn the corner and see the light at the end of the tunnel. I realized that I had allowed so many false beliefs to bottle me up and keep me from expressing myself even to God. I found out that it is totally acceptable to be angry as long as I have boundaries of expression—like no violence and no lashing out at the other person to hurt them with my words or actions.

God intends that I experience life fully and enjoy being the person He created me to be. I learned that my self-worth is in what God says about me—not in what other people think of me. As the chains of bondage fell from me and my soul was set free by my new belief system, I felt true joy begin to return to my heart. God enveloped me in His love and restored my hope. He is truly a very present help in time of trouble.

Soon after coming home from my six-week stay in the hospital, I was still very tender. Yet I was beginning to understand that I was a man greatly loved by God—not merely a pastor living in that role. I wrote some very meaningful Scriptures in my diary along with some of the conversations I had with God. These verses continue now to express my joy and thanksgiving to God's sustaining grace in my life.

> You turned my wailing into dancing; You removed my sackcloth and clothed me with joy that my heart may sing to You and not be silent; O Lord my God, I will give You thanks forever.
> (Psalm 30:11-12)

> I will be glad and rejoice in your love, for you saw my affliction and knew the anguish of my soul. You have not handed me over to my enemy but have set my feet in a spacious place.
> (Psalm 31:7-8)

> Be strong and take heart all you who hope in the Lord.
> (Psalm 31:24)

I prayed this brief prayer to God after reading the above Scriptures: "Father, I rely on you alone for my strength and complete recovery—in Your time. Thank You for sustaining me these past six weeks! May you strengthen Joan during these days. I do love you, my King!"

Coming Apart at the Seams

As a part of our recovery, we spent a week in the mountains of Tennessee during the winter of 1989. In the chalet we were staying at, I found the following words written that spoke volumes to what my heart was crying out for, and I wrote "resting in Jesus" beside this writing in my diary. The title is "Slow Me Down Lord."

> Ease the pounding of my heart by the quieting of my mind. Steady my hurried pace. Give me, amidst the confusion of my day, the calmness of the everlasting hills. Break the tensions of my nerves, with the soothing music of the singing stream. Help me to know the restoring power of sleep. Teach me the art of slowing down to look at a flower; to watch a spider build a web; to read a good book. Remind me that there is more to life than increasing its speed. . .[1]

Finally before closing out this chapter, I wrote the following prayer January 8, 1989:

> Lord, thank You for this morning here up in the mountains of Tennessee. Thank You for causing me to realize I am to love my dear Jennifer with 'unconditional love' as well as Danny and David. I came here to have my heart warmed by God's limitless love and realize that my family is my greatest ministry. Thank You Lord for allowing me now to redeem the time I have remaining with my precious children.

Looking back on those days just described, while coming apart at the seams was extremely difficult and humbling; both of us have learned some lessons that will stay with us for the rest of our lives. Let's take a look at the lessons learned.

Chapter 6
Lessons Learned

I have truly come to embrace the very painful experiences from my past as welcome contributors that have molded my present and will aid the way I think and live in the future. At the time when I thought everything in my life was shutting down, there was certainly not one ounce of "embracing." That was true; everything was shutting down. But it was necessary so that a new blossom could bloom that would have never come forth because of the former false beliefs that would have choked out any new and fresh developments in my life.

The lessons learned back then are still (I am happy to say), being lived out today. By my power, *no*, but by the grace and power of the Lord Jesus Christ who guides me daily through the Person of the Holy Spirit and the Word of God. I have learned and am continuing to learn that only when we die to all that is about us, do we live to God above us.

While that process is painful, the outcome is delightful. My intimacy with God and those around me has taken on a whole new dimension. I have absolutely *no desire* to go back to those burdens and false beliefs that I chose to live under. While the temptations still arise, and at times I may drift back, the change that my God has brought about in my mind and lifestyle is absolutely fantastic. Are things now wonderful all of the time? No! But, my responses to life's challenges are much different.

Come on inside my private world for a few moments as I share some of the lessons learned that have made and are still making positive impacts on my life and on the people God allows to come across my path.

I am a living testimony that God's Word is true. "For nothing is impossible with God" (Luke 1:37). Although at the time, things may appear to be impossible, those impossible situations provide God with another opportunity to demonstrate His awesome power. I have also been blessed over and over again to know and experience first hand that, "the name of the Lord is a strong tower; the righteous run to it and are safe" (Proverbs 18:10).

One of the many lessons I learned throughout this journey was that the blame game never resolves anything and often leads to masking the real problem and a lack of ownership of one's responsibility. A key word that both Joanie and I learned during those days we received counsel was *choices*. The choices we make will lead to consequences in our lives and, at times, consequences in the lives of others. We are the ones that are responsible for the choices that we make.

Another giant lesson I learned was that living under a system of false beliefs will lead to confusion, pain, and continually unresolved issues in our lives. Throughout my recovery from clinical burnout, which began in 1988, I was taught to recognize the lies that I was then living under by the light of the truth of God's Word exposing those lies. God has provided the means to deliver each of us from whatever system of false beliefs we have lived under with the truth and power of His Word. As I was drawn away from the need for the approval of others, I was finding myself drawn closer to the Heart of God. I began to understand for the first time in my life that the size of an audience, the applause or criticism of others, the expectations that were self-imposed or received from others, would no longer be allowed to rule my life.

I would then and will continue for the rest of my life to live unto and serve an Audience of One! This Audience is God Himself! He is the One that I will stand before to give an accounting of my life. He is the One who gave all in the life of His Son Jesus, so that I might live forever. It is what God thinks of me that truly matters.

Although God designs what we go through, we decide how we go through it! Once again this brings us back to choices. I am fully persuaded that the best protection against Satan's lies is to know God's truth. To go a step beyond this is to live daily in the choice to live according to God's truth. For this to happen effectively, the Word of God must be in me so that I can recognize God's truth from Satan's lies. I believe this principle can and will free many people who also have lived under false beliefs and Satan's lies.

I wonder how many people are involved in situations or even relationships that they really do not desire, but continue in for all the wrong reasons. Must I always say the right thing? Am I associating with the right people? What are they thinking of me? What are they saying? How am I coming across to others? I am thrilled that our God does not get impressed by these things but simply desires our love! This frees me from the need to be associated with the right people for the wrong reason. My goal in life is no longer to look good but for the Lord Jesus Christ to look good through me and not because of me.

Several years ago while in counseling during our recovery time, I received some excellent counsel that I have continued to see come true. My counselor told me, "Bob, if you are serious about making some changes in your life for yourself, there will be those around you that you know who will not like these changes." I asked him why, and he proceeded to tell me, "They liked the old you because you did what they wanted and it served their purposes. Now that you will be changing (no longer living to please people), they will wish that you stayed the way you were."

This made a great deal of sense to me as those whom I had lived to please were simply following the pattern I had set for them. Now that I was convinced that there was certainly a better way to live, I would need to deal with people who expected of me what I no longer would be providing. The risk has been worth taking as I am living proof today that serving God and living to please Him brings about balance and true joy in one's life.

As I close out my portion of this chapter, look with me at the progress that was being made as I wrote the following in my journal dated February 18, 1993:

> "But the plans of the Lord stand firm forever, the purposes of his heart through all generations" (Psalm 33:11). Am I now trying to win the approval of men or of God? Or am I trying to please men? If I were still trying to please men, I *would not* be a servant of Christ (Galatians 1:10). Amen! I must be reminded of this Lord Jesus! Thank You so much! It is a wonderful truth to know and live, that God is with us in the darkness just as surely as He is with us in the light!

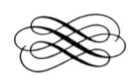

Lessons Learned

The life of bondage that I, Joan, had been living that had led me to depression was lonely and devastating to my soul. As God removed the blinders from my eyes, I was able to allow His healing to take place in my emotions and in my mind. It was here in the heart of me that I needed to be restored, for depression leaves behind emptiness and losses that need to be filled. Who better to do that than my Creator, the Author and Finisher of my faith, my Father God? So I willingly became the child, the student in the school of learning and healing by the power and anointing of the Holy Spirit within me (which continues to this day). God continued what He had started in the treatment center, and now I had the difficult task of putting into practice what He had begun.

He showed me freedom of expression. I remember in one of my sessions with my therapist, he told me that all my life I had not counted. I was always there for my family when I was growing up. As the firstborn, I was given a lot of responsibility with my three younger sisters. I did what I was told because I wanted to show them I could do a good job. I realized through these sessions with my therapist that my feelings and thoughts were never expressed. I was given a task and I did it. I had never "shown up," meaning I had never really voiced what I thought, liked, and felt about life and the things that were asked of me.

I began to "show up" once I went back home with my family. I realized that sharing my feelings and thoughts with my husband was much better than keeping them all bottled up inside me. I began to experience a closer relationship with my husband and my children. Our home, after a while, was released from constant tension and the feeling of walking on eggshells because feelings were shared and not stored up or overlooked.

Healthy expression was a welcome change from the way I lived before, never saying what I thought. I found that by simply stating "I am angry" or "I disagree" was enough. These things came slowly, and it wasn't always easy to express. Sarcasm still found its way out of my mouth when I was angry. There were many times I had to apologize. Through the years, I have found sharing how you feel is the best way and the honest way to interact with people.

God's truths continued to bring peace to my heart and build up my inner woman. I found that I experienced feelings like joy and happiness I had never known before. God created us with emotions to feel and enjoy life. By stuffing my feelings, I not only held down the negative ones, I also was not able to really experience the positive ones like happiness and love. Once I started being current with my feelings and allowing them healthy expression, I laughed more and smiled from down deep inside myself.

This is the part of the healing when the losses were restored to me. My soul was finding release in true joy. The insecure feeling I carried around inside myself since I was a little girl was at last finding security and confidence in God's love. As God's Word came alive in my life, I wrote the following thoughts as God spoke to my heart:

> I am God who is alive and powerful. My Word alone is sharper than any two-edged sword.
> Only in Me is there life.
> There is only wisdom and satisfaction in knowing Me.
> I am your God.
> I want you for Myself.
> Come onto Me and Me only.
> When you realize that your life is not your own,
> When you fully, completely rest in Me,
> Only then will you know peace and life.

For in Me only is there fullness of joy; only at My right hand are there pleasures forevermore.
You cannot be perfect.
You cannot know virtue and pure, holy love until your life is hidden in Me.
You cannot live My life by understanding, hours of Bible study, and trying your best to obey and do what is right.
No, it is not by might or by power but by My Spirit said the Lord of hosts.
Not until you lay down your all—your desires, your will, your controls—and give up, can I live in you.
Now My Spirit can take control—now you are truly My dwelling place—now you can rest, and My Spirit can live in you,
Begin to move and have My very being in you, transforming you, renewing you by the renewing of your mind, changing your thoughts—
For your thoughts are not My thoughts, but that doesn't mean they cannot be.
For you are My Beloved, My Bride, and I long to commune with you and to fellowship deeply with the inner you, My workmanship
And then I can begin to open up your eyes,
Let you understand the deeper things in life.
Then you will realize who you are in Me and how much I love you.
In your weakness I am your strength. I desire you to stay close to Me for I am a jealous God
And your weakness keeps you constantly seeking Me.
So you will only know strength, peace, joy and confidence as you abide in Me.
So look only unto Me, the Author and Finisher of your faith, and you will never lack anything ever again.
For it is My responsibility to see your life to completion—not yours.

As I write this down, I realize I am still living the truth of these words today and that I may never be able to completely live this way but it is to be my goal everyday of my life. I don't have to be hard on myself if I don't live up to a certain standard. There is such a peace and relief to find out that this life is not the struggle I made it out to be.

Life, as God intended it, is complete and utter dependence on God the Holy Spirit. The only reason I struggle is because my humanity wants to be in control and be noticed. It goes against the grain to let the Holy Spirit be in charge and live by faith. I am realizing the secret is being willing to say, "I cannot live this way Lord. I give up." I will say more about that in a future chapter. I am just thrilled that this is reality and that I can abandon myself into the hands of my loving Heavenly Father and not struggle anymore.

I am learning to let Him lead me. I used to live under such a sense of guilt which I am sure helped me into my depression. One of the most freeing lessons I learned was that God's way is not guilt but repentance that leads us to forgiveness, freedom, and peace. I walked around with a feeling that I never measured up; I always missed the mark. God brought home the marvelous truth that in Him I am blameless and completely loved. As a result of Jesus' sacrifice on the cross, God sees me as holy and blameless before I ever had a chance to sin. In His great love, He adopted me before I was ever born and made me His child. As I let this powerful truth in Ephesians 1 sink into my mind and heart, I am deeply relieved, secure in my life in Christ. My guilty feelings that weighed me down are a thing of the past. This is for me joy unspeakable and full of glory! It definitely puts a song in my heart and causes me to fall deeply in love with my God. No one on earth can walk into my life and do the marvelous things that He has done for me. He is truly my Hero.

Lessons Learned

I think my children must have been the happiest when their mother came home with the word *choices* forever on my lips (except maybe when I came home with our dog, Snowball). I was no longer so boxed in with my feelings, so my decisions were made with greater freedom.

I had been so quick to say *no* all the time whenever asked anything. It was always my first reaction. Now, I didn't want to say *no*, I wanted to say *yes* as much as I could to whatever they asked. You know, they say in therapy that when you are getting better the pendulum swings way over to the other side, well, it is completely true in my case. I was so boxed in for so long that the freedom of choices was so wonderful, I went way over on the other side for a while before finding the balance right in the middle of the two.

My daughter and I enjoyed each other more in conversation and hanging around together. I had more fun with the boys as well. I think I drove my husband crazy for a while but things settled down as choices became the norm. It was difficult at first when they were used to me acting one way and then I changed.

It took lots of mistakes, communication, and space to work through our new ways of relating. We kid now that you never have to wonder where I am at; I will let you know how I am feeling and what I am thinking. Learning to trust my husband with my feelings has been the best thing in the world for me. I know him better, and he knows me better. He is truly my best friend, and I can tell him anything. It is possible to walk closely with someone and feel isolated even when you are with them. My decision to trust him and let him into my heart has blessed my life so much.

It was never Bobby's fault. I married a very warm and sensitive man who has always been kind and loving to me. It was my fears of being vulnerable and then of being rejected that kept me from sharing my heart. I wouldn't take the chance. I learned that sharing your innermost thoughts with someone who loves you is safe and rewarding. God has helped me to grow stronger in myself through Bobby's patience, kindness, and sticking with me when life got difficult. I know that it was God that supplied this love and acceptance for me in my relationship with my husband. "Every good and perfect gift is from above, coming down from the Father of the heavenly lights" (James 1:17).

My approach to life definitely changed because my perspectives had been renewed. Problems still existed, but my outlook on them was not the same. I had the freedom to see my difficulties as challenges to be overcome. I thank God for allowing this breakdown into my life and using it to get my attention because it helped me handle other experiences in my home that would have completely devastated me. God is wisdom, and He knows the beginning and the end of our story. He does all things well for His glory and our best. Our welfare is always first and foremost with Him.

I would like to end my part in this chapter with this prayer to God that He gave me to write. This prayer comes from my heart that is forever grateful to my Creator for loving me enough not to leave me the way I was but to change me and continue to make me more like Him. God's Word tells us in John 10:10b that Jesus came that we may have life and have it to the full. This is my prayer to my Father God who released me from my box mentality and gave me freedom in choices, which took me away from rules and regulations and showed me life in grace and mercy. The change is miraculous and is accomplished by the awesome power of the Holy Spirit as He transforms our minds. (Romans 12:2) In my case, He showed me that He is limitless, and I am to follow Him not the other way around. Now my heart overflows and may you be blessed as we praise our Mighty God together with this prayer:

O, Jesus I love You. You are eternal, great, and mighty. Your Name cannot be equaled. You are holy, majestic, and righteous. You are power, glory, and strength. There is none like You. You reign supreme in truth and justice. Everything You do is perfect and right. With You there are no mistakes, no faults. You can be completely trusted and You cannot be put in a box. You are limitless.

I fall down in the awesome, overwhelming Presence of the almighty, pure Lamb of God. Only because of Your generous love and mercy do I have the privilege of calling You Lord and Savior.

Thank You that You have chosen to use fallen man to glorify Your Name. Thank You for becoming the unblemished Lamb who willingly sacrificed *all* so that I may live a life full of joy and be a child of the King of Kings.

I desire to walk in submission, in obedience to Your holy will. I do not want to go my own way and may I forever keep in my mind that I am but dust so that I may walk in the love of Jesus Christ and be a blessing to all I meet. So use me—*use me*—or I have no reason for living.

Thank You, God, that I see Your purposes fulfilled in my life. In the relationships with my husband and children, through them I see Your plan for me in life. Just as You flung the sun, moon, and stars in their positions in the great universe and set them in orbit, You created me, breathed life into me, and set your plan for me in motion. You are in the process of fulfilling Your purposes in me. May I keep on my knees with my eyes on You lest I miss out on something You desire to do through me.

Isn't God wonderful! He is not a taskmaster. He is our loving, heavenly Father. I can trust this wonderful God. He has so much to teach me as I remain in His school of experiencing Him. God desires to establish my husband and me to help us possess the land like He did for the children of Israel. We are His children, and we are depending on Him.

God never lets us down, and He desires our well being so He has shown us another marvelous truth to keep us safe and protected—the freedom of boundaries.

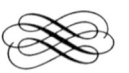

Chapter 7

The Freedom of Boundaries

Although the title, "The Freedom of Boundaries" may sound like a contradiction, there truly is great freedom in making choices for yourself that set personal limitations for your own benefit. For example, I used to spend as much as two to three hours with people in counseling without setting limitations. I allowed their need to dictate the length of our sessions. By setting limits ahead of time, we now have a clear understanding of the goals for our sessions without trying to accomplish too much at one time. By choosing healthy and balanced limitations in all areas of life, I now set reasonable goals and do not live under others' expectations. As a man who used to live without boundaries at all, I have welcomed this change in both my personal and professional life. And it is working! It is so refreshing to accept the fact that I am not the answer to everybody's need. There is only One Savior, and His name is Jesus Christ!

There is great joy and liberty in submitting to the only One who is capable to guide me and who knows me entirely.

To submit to the opinions and expectations of others, puts us in bondage and steals our joy. I learned a great truth along the way regarding the importance of how we live: "If you don't live by what is above you, what is below you will pull down what is in you."

God has taught me to seek Him first before making decisions. There are many times when saying *no* is a good thing. By seeking God's blessing I must commit myself to be quiet and hear from Him. There is ample provision in God's Word that He has already given to direct our lives. At times, people around us may not like or agree with our choices, but remember Who it is we are serving! You see, if we live for the approval of God, we may receive the disapproval of men.

I believe there is a place for healthy expectations. As I began to practice this new way of thinking I came to the conclusion that I can expect much from the Creator and little from the creature. Only God Himself can come through one hundred percent of the time. Although His ways are not our ways, I would rather trust myself completely to His ways rather than to man's ways. By placing limits on what I expect from men, my disappointments in and with others decreases as I accept their limitations and welcome them (as well as myself) back into the human race.

I have seen the setting of boundaries work as I began to tell people ahead of time in counseling how much time I had to give them. They became aware of the time constraints as I asked them how they wanted to use their time for that session. It became easier and easier with practice, and people respected the boundaries as I consistently upheld them. I can also remember times when I was asked to serve on committees, take on new responsibilities, or give extra time to new projects. As I weighed my options, I enjoyed the freedom that accompanied the choices that I made

The Freedom of Boundaries

without guilt or obligation. The freedom of boundaries is working in my life.

I am learning the great value of being able to say no without taking on guilt for being honest. Setting my boundaries in advance means that I do not have to explain them later. What a relief has come to this man who never would say *no* to anyone for any reason. As this approach is working, there is no need to give my reasons for my answer, but there is freedom to simply state my answer. I used to become frustrated by taking on more things than I could effectively be involved in, but failed to say *no* because I saw my worth in those activities.

As I am learning to set boundaries in my life, I am becoming more aware of my own limitations. Rather than seeing those limitations as obstacles to overcome, I have accepted them as friends to be recognized. I am now free to do some things well, and I no longer attempt to do all things. This releases me from being result oriented as I am learning that I am not responsible for results, but I am responsible to obey.

Although the truth is liberating, at times it may be painful. While writing this chapter, I found myself saying the following statement out loud that may be of some benefit to you: "Some of the hardest truths to accept are those things we know are true about ourselves that we don't like to hear, and yet we must come to face them as real." When examined honestly, this process will ultimately lead to freedom. We can admit to God and ourselves what our condition is and then become a candidate for change through the working of the Holy Spirit in our lives.

I wrote the following observations in my journal during the winter of 2000: "Human control insists on immediate results; God's control allows for a lifelong process of change. To be under Christ's control is to have true freedom!" Someone else has said, "When we can't see God's Hand, we can trust His Heart!"

As each of us comes to accept change as a lifelong process, we shed the self-imposed chains of bondage like setting dates (telling God how and when to fix us), making projections regarding the future, and trying to help God out by directing the course we think He should be taking in our lives. Wow! What a relief! Why not try this refreshing and life-changing way of thinking and living. Our God can be trusted! How about trusting Him to do what we have not been able to do thus far, as we move over and allow the true King of Kings and Lord of Lords to have His rightful place in our lives?

One of the practical aspects about establishing boundaries in our lives is that in setting our own limits we then become aware of what we are responsible for and can concentrate on those areas. These clear boundaries, once established, help us to clearly recognize what our responsibilities are so that we can take care of those things and not cross over into other people's business or responsibilities.

The term "stay in your own skin" has been most helpful to me in this process. I have plenty on my own plate to enjoy and be responsible for; therefore, the more I stay in my own skin the less I will be concerned with what others are doing and the way they are doing those things. This also frees me from becoming judgmental as I concentrate on the needed changes in my own life.

As we learn to set limits and accept our own responsibilities, boundaries become welcome friends for life. One of the nice things about setting boundaries is that you can change them as you need to, because they are yours. Setting boundaries is a great way to get order and balance in our lives. They provide us with open doors of freedom as we

The Freedom of Boundaries

decide what boundaries to live by, and we adjust our lives accordingly to what works for us.

What a great impact the practice of setting boundaries has made on my life. There is freedom in setting boundaries, because they draw a line of distinction between what is pertinent and what is superfluous. Instead of being spread out all over the place and running around like a chicken with my head cut off or having my hands into more than I can handle, I can pull back, say *no*, and be more effective in what I do need to accomplish.

In placing limitations on myself, I am able to feel good about what I do get involved with, instead of doing things because I should or because no one else is going to do it and it (whatever "it" is) just has to get done. When I reasoned like that, I felt powerless and at the mercy of others to set my boundaries. I would feel like it was not my choice. My involvement would become a chore rather than a delight. Did you ever notice how different you feel when you are doing something you made the choice to do? No matter how challenging or difficult the task can become, I feel energetic and enthusiastic about my involvement because I want to be there.

Setting boundaries puts me in control of my life. I make the decision based on the criteria I want to use and the Holy Spirit can lead me into where I will be involved. As I see it, there is enjoyment and satisfaction when I approach a situation or try to determine what I will do with my time. No one is setting my agenda without my permission. I will feel good about myself with a great sense of satisfaction after my task is accomplished.

When I choose to say *no*, I don't have to feel guilty for long because I am doing the best I can and there is always someone else who can do the job or it doesn't have to get done. I believe that setting boundaries helps me establish my priorities. I realize I cannot do everything even if it is a good thing. As I set limits, it helps me to take care of myself. Then I can take care of my family, get involved in the church, and keep my life in order.

Setting boundaries not only helped in establishing my time, it has also helped in my people relationships. In the church, I was honest about my feelings, what I could be involved with, and how I shared my thoughts. In my home, I shared my thoughts more with my husband about how I felt about situations in our home. I no longer feared what his reactions might be or if my thoughts might rock the boat.

I would be honest, and in sharing I would say how I would like to be treated. I learned that how I allow people to speak to me and interact with me on a daily basis is important. I learned there are healthy limitations on how people should approach each other and speak to each other. It is important to let people know how they come across in conversation. Respect needs to be given to one another.

Over all this boundary setting, I place myself under the love and grace of God, desiring that my reactions be pleasing to Him. I must always remember that God tells me to love another as I love myself. So, I will treat others the way I would like to be treated and be guided by the Holy Spirit.

As our lives continued to be established on a new foundation of thinking and living, we were finding a new dimension in family living that was changing the atmosphere in our home. We became more aware of the fun and laughter in life and found that our joy was being restored.

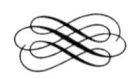

Chapter 8
Joy Restored

When the awesome power of God's love transforms the inside of a person, the outer expression of that love is bound to break out sooner or later. One of my earlier characteristics both as a pastor and also in my family life was that at times I was too intense for my own good (and also for the good of those around me).

I can recall someone saying to me (one of those truths I did not like to hear but was true), "Pastor Bob, when you first came to our church you smiled more, but now you are serious all of the time." As God continued working on my heart, my motives began to change, and I gave myself permission to be relaxed with myself and enjoy people and the beauty of God's creation once again. I will admit that this area of my life is still under construction, as intensity seems to be a characteristic that flows frequently from my life. While I believe that intensity can be a blessing, it needs to be a part of my life and no longer the primary focus of my life.

As I was realizing how God was changing me, I wanted to share His love with other people along the way. I wrote in my journal, "In complete dependence on you, Lord Jesus, let me relay Your message of love and peace to the desperate and needy souls that I meet." One of the wonderful ways that God used to restore my joy was with a fresh love for His Word and through a life of praise. One morning after being captured by a taste of the Glory of God as portrayed in Revelation four and five I wrote:

> This morning God, Your glory is awesome. You are great, majestic, and holy. I praise Your name forever and ever! All that the twenty-four elders could do was to fall down and worship You! Can I do any less? Glory to my God and King and Savior!

I can testify to the absolute truth that is stated in Isaiah 49:23b, "Those who hope in me will not be disappointed." I am so blessed to both know and experience that God is always there regardless of my feelings and throughout my disappointments in life.

Charles Swindoll wrote:

> Candidly, I know of nothing that has the power to change us from within like the freedom that comes through grace. It's so amazing it will change not only our hearts but also our faces. And goodness knows some of us are overdue for a face change! Were you raised by parents whose faces said "No"? Or are you married to someone with a "No" face? If that is true, you envy those who had "Yes"-face parents or are married to "Yes"-face mates. All of us are drawn to those whose faces invite us in and urge us on.[1]

Having been one of those "No"-face parents and "No"-face husbands, I still to this day am learning from those who do a much better job than I at showing a "Yes"-face. Who are they? My wife, Joan and my three children, Danny, Jennifer and David, who have taught me and are continuing to teach me by their example to have a "Yes"-face.

My family means the world to me, and I desire to be more like each of them in this area. I wanted to share that personal example of my growing need along the way before continuing with the following story.

During his days as president, Thomas Jefferson and a group of companions were traveling across the country on horseback. They came to a river that had left its banks because of a recent downpour. The swollen river had washed the bridge away. Each rider was forced to ford the river on horseback, fighting for his life against the rapid currents. The very real possibility of death threatened riders, which caused a traveler who was not part of their group to step aside and watch. After several had plunged in and made it to the other side, the stranger asked President Jefferson if he would ferry him across the river. The president agreed without hesitation. The man climbed on, and shortly thereafter the two made it safely to the other side. As the stranger slid off the back of the saddle onto dry ground, one in the group asked him, "Tell me, why did you select the president to ask this favor of?" The man was shocked, admitting he had no idea it was the president who had helped him. "All I know," he said, "is that on some of your faces was written the answer 'No,' and on some of them was the answer 'Yes.' His was a 'Yes' face."[2]

The reason that I love this story so much is that as my joy was in the process of being restored, it would also appear on my face, in my attitudes, and in my actions.

As my joy was being restored, I learned to laugh again. One of the best things that a serious person like myself can do is to laugh at himself. What a joy it has become to enjoy life again. To enjoy God and my family and friends is a wonderful gift that I value and am growing in daily.

When mistakes are made, I find myself owning them sooner. God gave me back my love for people and His Work. The difference being that when things are in balance they all take on a new perspective and purpose in life. I began to look forward to ministry again with renewed joy and vision. I saw my family in a new light as they were now in practice a priority in my life. My life with God is becoming more intimate as I am spending much more time listening to Him than I used to. When I am quiet before My Father, I am taken into His Presence in which there is fullness of joy!

As God spoke to the Israelites in the Old Testament, I was blessed, as I believe He pours out His affection on me as He did so often on them. Rejoice with me in the following Scripture from Deuteronomy 7:7-9:

> The Lord did not set affection on you and choose you because you were more numerous than other peoples, for you were the fewest of all peoples. But it was because the Lord loved you and kept the oath he swore to your forefathers that he brought you out with a mighty hand and redeemed you from the land of slavery, from the power of Pharaoh king of Egypt. Know therefore that the Lord your God is God; he is the faithful God, keeping his covenant of love to a thousand generations of those who love him and keep his commands.

God has redeemed me from my slavery of people-pleasing, unrealistic expectations, living to work, and being driven beyond measure. My heart leaps for joy as God Himself has done a marvelous work in my life. People are the heart of God's Heart. His Son, Jesus Christ did not die for programs, strategies, or plans. He died for people, He rose again for people, and He now intercedes for people. I have come to love God in a greater way and as a result, He has given to my heart a true love for His Creation. Once again I am in awe of His greatness.

I picked up the following statement along the way that has given me a new motivation for service: "Real love is helping someone for Jesus' sake who can never return the favor." Did not our Lord Jesus Christ do that very thing for us? I am compelled to give that kind of love to others and to give it with great joy. God loves His People as is stated in Jeremiah 31:13:

> Then maidens will dance and be glad, young men and old as well. I will turn their mourning into gladness; I will give them comfort and joy instead of sorrow."

That is the goodness of God! There is absolutely *nothing* beyond the capability of God. Will you not come to trust Him as I have for the great needs in your life? After all, He is the One who made you and knows how to put your life back together. Listen to the question that God poses to Jeremiah in chapter 32, verse 27: "I am the Lord, the God of all mankind. Is anything too hard for me?" No! No! No! Nothing is too hard for our God! This broken, restored life is living proof, and He will do the same for you if you allow Him to do it in His way and in His time.

Before Joanie continues this chapter, I want to leave you with what I wrote in my journal on June 20, 2001: "Lord, thank You for reminding me of the first priority— Abiding in You. Intimacy with You. The worship of You.

Fellowshipping together and loving each other." Psalm 9:10 declares: "Those who know your name will trust in you, for you, Lord, have never forsaken those who seek you."

My heart cannot praise God enough as I share the heart of David in Psalm 13:5,6: "But I trust in your unfailing love; my heart rejoices in your salvation. I will sing to the Lord, for he has been good to me." The reason I share so much Scripture with you is that it is God's Word! He alone produces anything of lasting value. He alone restores my soul. He alone is to receive *all* the glory!

I have experienced first hand what is declared in Psalm 35:18: "The Lord is close to the brokenhearted and saves those who are crushed in spirit." As I write this final Scripture for this chapter, I am smiling and weeping with tears of joy and eternal gratitude, as I know that what God has done for me He can do for you. Will you open your heart to the warmth of His all-consuming love? Psalm 30:11,12: "You turned my wailing into dancing; you removed my sackcloth and clothed me with joy, that my heart may sing to you and not be silent. O Lord my God, I will give you thanks forever."

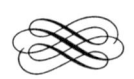

I, Joan, rejoice in the fact that God is good and that His love endures forever. God used my depressions to heal my inner life. What I would have thought was awful and cruel, God has used for His glory and my good. As I heal and exercise the changes in my life, even my worst moments are not as bad as before.

I know it is because I have learned to let go. I realized that letting God be in control is my way to true joy and freedom. Unexplainable joy and peace became a part of my life once I learned to let God be in control of my life. I experience all the pain and disappointments of life but differently than I did before. I found that my heart experiences my feelings to the fullest now that I am not ignoring them anymore.

Having gone through such a devastating breakdown, I now feel joy and happiness and have opened my heart to all my emotions. I enjoy my children more, and I share my thoughts and feelings with my husband more which all adds up to closer relationships since now I am not trying to hide myself. I am not trying to say the right thing in order to not hurt someone's feelings. I speak my thoughts about situations and want to share what I think about the church, or my home, or how a move may have affected me.

I would like to use the illustration of a parent and a child to convey the truths I learned that have restored my joy. It is in this picture that I see the child who is myself in relationship to the parent who is my Father God. The child can express herself because her parent will listen and love her, never condemn her or put her down. So this child has no need to wonder if she is loved. She knows, believes, and trusts her parent.

I know this is an ideal story, but it speaks to the total love and care that I experience with a perfect heavenly Father. I can let Him be in control. I have learned the secret of letting go, which is really no secret. It is just being a child, being submissive, and wanting God more than my own way. I truly believe He knows what is best for me, and I don't want to help Him out. I know I can't do any better.

When waiting or being a child gets tough, I get to tell Him. I don't walk a tightrope of trying to do the right thing anymore. He helps me to know peace and quietness right in the midst of uncertainties and difficulties because He is greater than my greatest difficulty or my worst fear. I am learning what is His responsibility and what is mine. He is completely dependable and will never let me down. I will never be rejected or abandoned by Him so my heart is free to be joyful and at peace. I want to keep my hand in my Father's hand and trust Him with my life. This is true joy.

God has restored my joy in realizing His total acceptance of me. In Romans 8:1, I read, "Therefore, there is now no condemnation for those who are in Christ Jesus." I know what it is to love myself and accept myself so that I can truly love others. I have learned to recognize the enemy's attacks and his subtle, deceptive thoughts. Therefore, I no longer dwell in condemnation.

I know that God loves me and will enable me to love others from a full and contented heart. I can pass this on to my children, to my husband, and to my friends by the way I enjoy life with them and love them unconditionally even when difficult situations come along. I believe that together we can face the most difficult circumstances life has to throw at us because underneath us are the loving arms of Almighty God.

One afternoon I received a call from a lady asking me if I would consider being the speaker at a mother/daughter banquet. After praying, I called her back and said that I would be honored to speak to the women on the theme of hope. As I wrote down the thoughts that I would share, I realized what an impact hope has made in restoring my joy. I would like to share my thoughts with you:

> I had lived through a very hopeless time in my life, so having hope back in my heart had greatly changed my perspectives for the better. I am excited to know that God has given us a hope for the future in giving us His son, Jesus Christ, to die on the cross for our sins. As a result of His death and resurrection, we have hope, not

only in the future but in the present as well. The truth definitely affects how we live because it gives us assurance and peace, which leads to joy. It reminds me of the words to a song that God gave me after going through my trial, "God is my Rock. He is my sure foundation. No one can harm me for God is my Rock. Trials may come my way and friends leave my side, but my eyes will not leave Jesus for God is my Rock. My security is not in this world, my heart's treasure's in Heaven and God is my Rock." We can count on God. He will not let us down. He will not fail us.

The world tells us that we are our hope. We grow up believing that the answers lie within us, that we can make a difference. I believe that many of our control issues come from this belief. As we strive to make a difference in our homes or our social settings, we try to control outcomes by setting standards we force ourselves or other people to meet. It is not natural in the human element to allow the Holy Spirit to work out situations in our lives; at least it wasn't for my life.

I have come to believe that we can make a difference but only as we fully surrender our lives to God. He makes the difference in us, and, therefore, in the world. Christ says that He is our hope—without Him we can do nothing. In Proverbs 3:5,6 we read, "Trust in the Lord with all your heart and lean not on your own understanding. In all your ways acknowledge Him and He will direct your paths." God says that we are not to trust in ourselves. So, I ask, then why do we? Why do we live like we are in control and that everything stops with us?

I believe Jesus wants to dwell deep within our hearts. He is a jealous God, and He wants to come inside our lives. He made you, and He knows you better than you know yourself. He wants you to give Him the very core of who you are—the woman deep inside yourself—way down there where no one sees. The real you.

Let's take a minute here, ladies. We all know that we have longings deep in our hearts in that part of you where hope dwells. If we are going to know true peace, joy, and contentment—not as the world gives but as God gives—then we have to let God in and surrender this part of us. God will then dwell in us by the power and might of the Holy Spirit.

We must allow Him to be in control and to help us make the decisions in our lives. You are "God's workmanship, created in Christ Jesus to do good works, which God prepared in advance for us to do" (Ephesians 2:10). You see, when He truly has room in our hearts to live and move and have His very being, then He can be our Hope (Acts 17:28). And we can follow Him and let Him show us the plans and purposes He has for you and me.

It is never too late to let Him in. In case you wonder or doubt if you can let go and let God be in charge of your life—if He will really be a God who cares for you, let me share this story in closing:

"Hawa Ahmed was a Muslim student in North Africa. One day, she read a Christian tract in her dormitory and decided to become a Christian. Her father was an Emir (Islamic ruler), so she expected to lose her inheritance because of her conversion. She was completely unprepared for what happened. When she told her family she had become a Christian and changed her name to Faith, her father exploded in rage. Her father and brothers stripped her naked and bound her to a chair fixed to a metal plate with which they wanted to electrocute her. Faith asked them to at least lay a Bible in her lap. Her father responded, "If you want to die together with your false religion, so be it." One of her brothers added, 'That will show that your religion is powerless.' Although they had bound her, she was able to touch a corner of the Bible. She felt a strange peace, as though someone were standing beside her. Her father and brothers pushed the plug into the socket—and nothing happened. They tried four times with various cables, but it was as though the electricity refused to flow. Finally her father, angry and frustrated, hit her and screamed, 'You are no longer my daughter.' "

Then he threw her into the street, naked. She ran through the streets, humiliated and in pain. People looked at her, curious rather than shocked. Shaking and tearful, she ran to a friend. Her friend let her in, clothed her, and gave her shelter. The next day, her friend asked neighbors whether they had seen Faith running naked through the streets. 'What are you talking about?' they asked. 'The girl had a wonderful white dress on. We asked ourselves why someone so beautifully clothed had to run through the streets.' God had hidden her nakedness from their eyes, clothing her in a beautiful white dress. Today, Faith is a full-time evangelist with Every Home for Christ."[3]

This is the kind of God we serve and you can bring yourself—that deep, dark, loneliest spot in your soul to God, and He will give you dignity, clothe you, love you, and give you hope. Psalm 146:5 states, "Happy are those who are helped by the God of Jacob. Their hope is in the Lord their God." Let this hope fill your heart.

This ended my talk with the ladies.

I would like to elaborate a little on why we live like we are in control. We tend to do what is most familiar to us. We are raised with trusting in ourselves, or maybe our life situations have taught us that people will let us down, so we had better take care of things in our own lives. We must learn that God is totally trustworthy. Perhaps the pain of abandonment or the fear of rejection has resulted and completely strangles you and keeps you from allowing God to be in control. The only way that I have come to find freedom and have the ability to let the Holy Spirit lead me is by bringing my deep pains and fears to the Lord and letting Him heal them and shine His light on my soul—His truth on my unhappy memories. He has the absolute power to heal and set us free from any experience that has left us broken and bleeding. He doesn't just put a Band-Aid on the wound; He heals the wound with no scab. His love is powerful, and His oil is the balm that brings us healing. We have to believe. We have to trust Him with the darkest part of our souls. If we do, He will walk into our hurt and love us, never condemn us, and free us from the lies that hold us captive to the fears and anxieties of today.

As I end this chapter, I would like to share these thoughts that the Holy Spirit impressed upon my heart and I titled it – Set Free to Be Me.

> I have released you to walk in newness of life. Do not worry that you will walk in bondage again, all tied up in rules and regulations. When the Holy Spirit sets you free you are free indeed. The old ways have died and behold all things have become new. Now I am fee to be me, God's workmanship created in His image.

As Bobby and I, individually and together, were having our joy restored by God, He was giving us beauty for ashes in our lives.

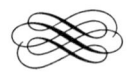

Chapter 9

Beauty for Ashes

I can remember talking with Joanie one day during our recovery as we asked ourselves the following question: "Do you think that God could use our story to help others some day?" Little did we know then that He would bring us out of the ashes of brokenness into the beauty of His marvelous light and healing.

We are recipients of God's grace and healing and have experienced the wonderful touch of the Lord as we went through the deep waters of despair for several months. The waves of discouragement, oppression of the enemy, downpours of doubt and fear came on each of us for a season.

At times it seemed as if there was no way out. Then God came and through His Holy Spirit brought a covering of peace over our hurt and confusion. We have been forever changed and healed by the Lord Jesus Christ. Throughout our journey, we have experienced and continue to live out daily the wonderful hope that is delivered by our Lord as is described in Isaiah 61:1-3:

> The Spirit of the sovereign Lord is on me, because the Lord has anointed me to preach good news to the poor. He has sent me to bind up the brokenhearted, to proclaim freedom for the captives and release for the prisoners, to proclaim the year of the Lord's favor and the day of vengeance of our God, to comfort all who mourn, and provide for those who grieve in Zion—to bestow on them a crown of beauty instead of ashes, the oil of gladness instead of mourning, and a garment of praise instead of a spirit of despair. They will be called oaks of righteousness, a planting of the Lord for the display of his splendor.

Every time I read this Scripture my heart is touched because of the greatness of God's healing.

I have learned that problems are opportunities to discover God's solutions. It is not my job to make things happen, but it is my responsibility to trust God. There are times when we are directed to go forward, and there are also times when God will have us stop in the direction that we are headed. It is actually a great blessing of God when, at times, He withholds from us that which we desire as He knows what is best suited for us at that very time in our life. Since He orders our steps and our stops, we can rest in His sovereignty and allow Him to truly be the Lord of our lives.

Whatever God desires is where my heart wants to be as He alone is the One that I want to follow. I have learned through the valley times of my darkest days that God's dawn of deliverance often comes when the hour of trial is the darkest. Why might that be so? Well, during those times there is absolutely nothing I can bring to the needed solutions.

It seems that when we are at our lowest, and have exhausted all that we know to do, God Himself carries us along through His sustaining grace. Psalm 50:15 speaks to this issue: "Trust in me in your times of trouble, and I will rescue you, and you will give me glory." It is God and God alone who carries us and heals our broken lives with the soothing oil of His Presence and the strength of His Power.

Revelation 21:1-7 wonderfully describes the New Jerusalem. God will make everything new, and I am looking forward with great anticipation to verse seven, which states, "He who overcomes will inherit all this, and I will be his God, and he will be my son." After reading that, I wrote in my journal during my recovery in 1990: "The glories of heaven will totally eclipse the trials of earth." My heart agrees with the declaration of David described for us in Psalm 40:5: "Many, O Lord my God, are the wonders you have done. The things you planned for us no one can recount to you; were I to speak and tell of them, they would be too many to declare." Wow! Isn't that the truth! When we hold things tightly, we do not realize the great potential that God has in store for us as He works with those who give Him their plans, families, futures, and lives. The only things we really lose are the things we try to keep. After all, are we not much better off in the Hands of our God than in our own hands?

My purpose in life is found in Ephesians 1:11-12:

> In him we were also chosen having been predestined according to the plan of him who works out everything in conformity with the purpose of his will, in order that we, who were the first to hope in Christ, might live for the praise of his glory.

That means in everything I do, I do it unto God. He is my reason and true motivation for service to other people. Living for the praise of God's glory affects all areas of our lives. The way we work, the way we play, the way we rest, our family life, all are for God. What a wonderful God I love and serve who took the ashes of my life and restored me for His glory.

Something very special happened within our family on November 17, 1989. There we were on our sixteenth wedding anniversary with our children, a few friends, and family members around us renewing our wedding vows. This was done as a testimony for what God had brought the entire Galasso family through by His grace. I would like to take you back to that day. It was a bright and windy day in south Florida. You are invited to listen to the vows Joanie and I shared with one another during that special service. Joanie said:

> Bobby, I want to tell you as we stand here today, I am happy to be renewing my vows to you. I am happy to be your wife, and I feel as if I am marrying you for the first time. I am so thankful, and I feel as if I have never loved you more than I do now, at this moment. I want to thank you for these sixteen wonderful years of marriage and let you know I appreciate the way in which you have taken care of me, you have honored and respected me, and have stuck by me, especially in the past year. Because of your love, which has proved itself unconditional, I stand here a changed person. God has used your life to bless me and at times to motivate me, to challenge me, and most importantly of all, to help me recognize how valuable I am. God has made the changes, and I thank Him for using you. I sincerely thank our Lord Jesus for giving you to me and for revealing His love for me through our relationship.

I said:

Joanie, eighteen years ago when I first met you in college, I knew you were very special. After one month, I knew I loved you. I thank my God for the beautiful gift He has given me in you! Throughout the last several years, I remember when there would be times when I would say, different people will come and go in our lives, and we will move to different places in the country. Things around us may change, but remember this: It's always going to be *you and me babe!*

I praise God that He works out everything in His time. My heart truly cries out with the psalmist:

Praise the Lord, O my soul; all my inmost being, praise his holy name. Praise the Lord, O my soul, and forget not all his benefits. He forgives all my sins and heals all my diseases; he redeems my life from the pit and crowns me with love and compassion. He satisfies my desires with good things, so that my youth is renewed like the eagle's.

(Psalm 103:1-5)

Every woman should believe that her husband is the best man in the world and that she is the luckiest girl in the world to be married to him. I feel that way about my husband and I am more than lucky, I am blessed by God with a kind and loving partner.

I can remember the day we were sitting at the table having lunch when he asked me to marry him again. I looked up at him and stared, I was speechless. We were seven months away from my hospitalization, and we had worked through a lot of changes; hard changes that could have spoiled our relationship. The pain and hurt that we experienced tested our love and commitment. At times in the adjustment of speaking up and placing boundaries, the emotions caused tensions and irritability. It took time and selflessness to hang in there and work things out. It would have been much easier to walk away. I know it was the grace of God and the fact that His arms were holding us that we did not succumb to the pressures in selfish ways.

We had plowed through the discomfort, and we had remained united. So here we sat, and there was my wonderful husband asking me to marry him again. I smiled and thought he was the most romantic man in the world and said, "Of course I will! What a wonderful idea!" Renewing our vows with another wedding ceremony would be just the way to declare before God and man that we were thankful to still be together and that God had brought beauty to us through the ashes of our depression and burnout.

I spent the next months getting ready for our anniversary/wedding. It was just what the doctor ordered. My heart and mind were able to think of joy and celebrating our lives. It helped me to replace the sorrow. It was like getting married all over again to the man of your dreams, the love of your life—your boyfriend. It was very healing for me.

There are few times in your life when you realize you are a part of something very special. This was how I felt on the day of our sixteenth wedding anniversary. In many ways, it added health and strength to our lives and deepened our commitment to remain together through the bad times as well as the good times.

I remember feeling like God was right there with His presence; His love for us was so strong. Our children and some very good friends were in the ceremony with us. The music and the flowers added more beauty to an already beautiful occasion. I know it was beneficial to the children to see their mom and dad smiling and happy with each other after seeing us separated and placed in hospitals.

We enjoyed the day so much. My friend invited us to use their home by the water. We gathered with family and friends along the river to say our vows. It was a beautiful day as we said *I do* again, and a loving, forever memory was created. I am thankful that God watched over us with His tender, loving care. He is a good Father, and we are blessed to be His children.

Having learned many lessons, seeing God restore our marriage, breathing fresh life into our weary souls, God was preparing to give us a fresh start. After all, He is the God of new beginnings. Now at this time in our life we would be starting over.

Chapter 10

Starting Over

Since leaving the ministry in the spring of 1989 (to care for my three children while my wife was in her recovery time), I went back to a trade that I had done all of my life. House painting came naturally to me, so I continued to do that as well as working with a local contractor, roofing and in the construction business.

Almost two years later, I wanted to enter back into the ministry as an evangelist within the district we were living in at the time. I was leading a Bible study at the racquetball club where I was working, and I was ready to get back into ministry again.

In the winter of 1991, I went before a committee of men who would consider my request to go into the work of evangelism. Throughout the lengthy interview, I was realizing that this call on my heart was not quite so obvious to them.

All my life up to that point in ministry, I had gladly submitted myself under the authority of those over me. No problem! On this particular afternoon, things were not going for me as I had hoped they would, and I was about to learn yet another lesson.

Throughout the interview, what I was hearing was not bringing joy to my heart. "Bob, you are still getting over your illness, and we do not think you are ready for this step." I thought I was already over my illness, so what were they talking about? As their questions and concerns came my way, I was not accepting what they were saying. "Bob, we believe you need more time, and we would like you to work under someone for a while as you enter back into the ministry." What were they saying? I had over seventeen years behind me! I could not believe what my ears were hearing.

I kept most of my feelings to myself, but the expression on my face could have sunk a ship. As I attempted to explain my calling and continued to share that I was feeling well and ready to jump right in again, the others in the room were not seeing things from my perspective. After about two hours, my request was unanimously denied. I was devastated! To make matters worse (or so I thought), they asked me to comply with their suggestion that I be an assistant pastor all over again. This was not going well with this forty-year-old veteran who had almost two decades of service at that time.

At the end of the meeting, one of the men, a pastor, said to me with a heart of compassion and grace, "Bob, I have a place for you here in our church if you would consider working with me." I looked into his eyes and knew he meant it. He really cared. I desperately needed to know that there was a place for me once again. I listened to his offer, knew it was for real, and considered my options.

I thanked the men and left for a thirty-minute ride home. With each minute, my feelings of doubt, rejection, failure, and anger grew stronger. As I entered my house, I told Joanie, "They said no! They want me to start all over again!" As she quietly listened (something she did often and quite well), my heart was broken by the Holy Spirit, and I immediately had a battle going on with my ego.

As one part of me asked, "How can I start all over again?" Another thought came to my mind that I attribute to the Holy Spirit of God. "You need this, Bob. You are not ready yet." Then I remembered the gracious offer that was set before me by that compassionate pastor and told Joanie I would accept.

The patience of God is marvelous! He knows just what we need and when we need it. God brings people into our lives just at the right time to say the right thing, which our wounded hearts need to hear.

I do not know about you, but in my life, *pride* is usually my number one sin. When it shows up, it rears its ugly head up high and needs to be put in its rightful place. Where is that? Under the submission and forgiveness of my Lord Jesus Christ.

Little did I know then that God would take another twelve years to prepare me to take a leap of faith and serve Him in ways I never thought of back then. He would also honor my desire to be an evangelist but not until He kept me in the school of humility, grace, and intimacy with Him for many years. That school is still going on today.

I accepted the offer to be an assistant pastor and was blessed with the pastor and congregation that God had graciously led me to. To this day, I am grateful for that "*no*" that has led to God's "*yes*" today. That story is soon coming later in this book. Remember how the "stops of a man are ordered by the Lord" as well as "his steps." Praise God for His perfect timing in all things.

During my ministry re-entry at that church I learned from the pastor the value of a personal vision statement. I had never considered the need for such a statement before and have since come to realize that in the years to come, the development and practice of that statement would provide me with a specific focus for ministry. After about two months of reading, prayer, and mentoring, I developed the following personal vision statement in the spring of 1991 which has served me well throughout the past eleven years:

> I believe God has called me to come alongside people and affirm them as they realize who they are in Jesus Christ. This will be accomplished as I recruit, train, and motivate lay people to use their God-given spiritual gifts in ministry.

This was one of the many reasons I needed to be mentored during this time in my life. You see, during the previous years in ministry I had no specific focus, so I shot arrows at many targets and tried to accomplish too many things. Now I was on track with God's calling, and I would prayerfully pursue that calling with new direction and purpose. I learned a great lesson that I entered in my journal in the spring of 1994: 1 Samuel 8:22: "The Lord answered, Listen to them and give them a king." (We know what happened under Saul's leadership.) Then I wrote: "Sometimes God allows us to have what we think we need! How much better to take from His Hand what we really need. What is better than seeking God alone?"

From that place of ministry, I would learn lifetime lessons. God led us to other places to serve Him and eventually in 1994 I would be called to pastor a church. Five and a half years in God's workshop would prepare me to preach once again, but this time I functioned differently as a pastor. I became a man of balance. I had other interests and was dedicated to my family.

During this process of starting over God truly brought healing and restoration into my life. The specific changes I made such as, regular days off, speaking honestly to those whom I had a problem with, setting boundaries, practicing the priority of family, and other changes would bring balance and order in my life.

The priority of my morning time with God grew both in time and in quality. He is my best Friend and knows my heart like no other.

My relationship with Joanie became closer because what God was doing in each of us separately added to the quality of our marriage and friendship. After the Lord, Joanie is truly the closest person to me. I also desired to be closer to my children and spend as much time as they would give to me. I enjoyed laughing again and looked forward to coming home. Although things were not perfect, I was doing much better on the inside. A new area for me was sharing the ministry with others. I enjoyed giving away responsibilities, where before I tried to do it all. Training leaders and enjoying their success brought joy and satisfaction to my calling.

During January of 1994, just before assuming a call to a new pastorate, my father passed away. I grieved for several months. My dad really loved my sister and me. He and my mom were married for over fifty-five years when he went home to be with our Lord. He taught me lessons that have stayed with me for life. To this day, I miss him dearly.

I thank God for a godly father and mother who created an atmosphere of love growing up where God was in our home. They taught me His love and read to me from His Word. My mom is still the greatest prayer partner I have. She goes to God on my behalf daily. I love my sister dearly and am blessed to have a family to love and to be loved by as they have been there for me throughout my entire journey.

A couple years into our new ministry I was under quite a bit of personal stress. Although I had continued to keep balance in my life, some personal things were becoming overwhelming. While attending a Promise Keepers event for some 40,000 pastors in Atlanta, Georgia, the following took place. I took the train downtown to the Georgia Dome where the event was happening, and as I got off the train I began to feel weak and dizzy. I made my way to the meeting but felt as if I was not doing well. After staying for a few minutes in my seat, I felt very sick. I sought help from the emergency personnel in the dome, and they placed nitroglycerin under my tongue and rushed me to Georgia Baptist Hospital.

I thought I was having a heart attack. After examining me, a cardiologist ordered a heart cauterization for the next morning. After signing a release (giving up all of my rights if I should die from the procedure), I made plans with my wife for the possibility of my departure from this life. I watched the procedure the next morning and found out that my arteries were clear. The doctor said I could leave later that day and told me to see my local physician.

On arriving home, I found out that I had ulcers brought on by stress. The symptoms were almost identical to a heart attack. Was that a wake up call? You bet! Joanie and I began walking a couple miles just about every day late in the afternoon. We've continued that practice during which we solve all of the world's problems as we talk, pray over our neighborhood, share our hearts and relieve some stress.

During the summer of 1998, I wrote this journal entry: "If the church I am involved in stops growing, I still give glory to God. If as a pastor, it means my leaving to make room for the next shepherd, God gets the glory. If it means my staying in spite of the odds, God gets the glory." It seems to me that the glory given to God is what really matters.

I came to understand that God knows our limitations and works through them. During those days, I learned to handle with care God's precious church. During that morning in my quiet time before God, I jotted down some notes that I thought might be encouraging to remember.

> As you serve God in whatever He has called you to do consider this: The foundation of ministry is character. The nature of ministry is service. The motive for ministry is love. The measure of ministry is sacrifice. The authority of ministry is submission. The purpose of ministry is the glory of God. The tools of ministry are the Word of God and prayer. The privilege of ministry is growth. The power of ministry is the Holy Spirit. The model of ministry is Jesus Christ.

God's plans for each of us are beyond what we think. The primary purpose of sharing our story with you is to encourage you to see the bigger picture and become Kingdom people for Christ. Hold on for the ride of your life. God has great plans for you.

> For I know the plans I have for you, declares the Lord, plans to prosper you and not harm you, plans to give you hope and a future. Then you will call upon me and come and pray to me, and I will listen to you. You will seek me and find me when you seek me with all your heart.
> (Jeremiah 29:11-13)

Starting over is never an easy time in anyone's life. It doesn't matter what the reason if you find that you must begin again. There are a lot of emotions and thoughts you have to deal with in order to begin the steps to setting up your life again. We needed the time away from certain responsibilities, but now we needed to get back into earning a living and being involved in ministering. God was placing this desire back into our hearts and we were ready.

As we looked around our home in Florida, we decided it was a good time to relocate to Georgia. We had no commitments to keep us in the town we were in, so we put our house for sale and moved to Stone Mountain, Georgia. Why did we pick this place? We thought it would be wonderful to move back to an area we loved and that felt like home. Also, my parents lived in Atlanta. This was a great place to start over and be around people we love and who love us.

One of the first things we did was find a church and start attending on a regular basis. It had been a long time since I had gone to church. Bobby and I found a church to attend as our children got acclimated to this new town and school.

Starting back to church turned out to be very difficult for me but very necessary. I found it extremely hard to sit in the pew without crying. I cannot explain the feelings that tumbled up into my heart and came down my face in tears throughout the whole service and particularly during the singing and preaching. There was a time when I decided it would be better not to go. Then as I thought it over, I realized that it was just what I needed to do no matter how difficult it was for me. I had to be healed, and this was God's way of restoring my losses and filling my emptiness. I was being cleansed and renewed and wholeness was just around the corner. If I fled this scene or bottled up my emotions, then I would just have to do it again later. What would be the point of that if I could be better by going through the tears?

So, I sat there crying Sunday after Sunday, and although I couldn't explain it, I felt better little by little, and one Sunday I wasn't crying anymore. I finally did get to the place where I could sit through a service without crying from hurt and pain. If I cried it was for other reasons as God dealt with my heart.

Sometimes we have to go through very difficult situations in order to be well emotionally. I have learned not to run from my pain or stuff my feelings, but stay and face the situation and, if I have to, learn from the difficulty, but never run from it. If I do stop my emotions, then I will not know the peace or contentment that can be mine by allowing the feelings to be expressed.

It was a hard experience but very healing and helped me to find my way back into church life and love the church again. I believe the tears ministered healing to my heart and helped me completely let go of all my hurt and resentments that I had from my experience in our breakdowns. It melted away all my false expectations. It freed me from any pain that was left by the disappointments.

God used this time to renew my heart, so He could replace the pain with true joy. By letting go of my false assumptions of the church, I was able to receive the truth of God's people loving and ministering healing to one another. Now I could put into practice that as God loves me, I can love you, and as I am free to be me, you are free to be you. In Christ, I am completely able to rest and accept people as they are—not as I would like them to be. This was just what I needed in order for God to bring us to the next step.

The day came when my husband decided to actively seek a position as an evangelist. It was a memorable occasion when Bobby pursued a place to minister again. My heart was thrilled and apprehensive as he made phone calls and set up an appointment to speak to a committee of men concerning his request. I couldn't help but wonder if we were ready. At the same time, I believed we were ready to begin ministry again. I had decided to support my husband, and I prayed for God's direction. He would provide for us and show us what to do. This is how I felt as the day of Bobby's appointment approached, and he left to meet with the committee.

I was crushed for my husband as he came home and shared that the committee did not believe he was ready to be an evangelist. I was disappointed for him because I knew he wanted this very much. Our consolation came from a pastor who offered him a position within his church. He wanted to help Bobby get back into ministry. I knew he needed a job, and as I thought about this situation, I realized this was just what God had planned for us at the very moment of Bobby's breakdown.

Our Lord knew we would have these breakdowns and need a time of recuperation. He provided for us, and He also knew that the day would come when we would re-enter the ministry. This was exactly His provision for us. As God brought this realization home to my heart, I began to praise Him for this pastor and this new church that we would go to.

The time spent in this church was such a blessing to our lives. God provided beautifully for our re-entry into the church. The friendships we formed in the days spent here in ministry are still a part of our lives today. God encouraged us through this body of believers, and we were able to grow in the principles and new concepts we had learned during our days of rebuilding our lives. In this atmosphere of positive working together in mutual love and respect, we became stronger in living out the ministry of loving and building people up in the kingdom of God.

Bobby learned to be more focused in ministry, and as I became friends with the pastor's wife and women of the church, I learned to be more open and secure in being vulnerable. Our children enjoyed this church and the friendships they made with kids their own age. Our God is a good God, and He not only takes care of mom and dad but He provides and cares for the children as well. We all benefited during this time. What we thought was so bad, God used for good in our lives.

God had established us back into ministry and now by His continued grace and guidance He would lead Bobby back to school.

Chapter 11
Back to School

During the spring of 1997, while attending our denomination's annual council, Joanie and I were casually walking through an exhibition area where booths were set up promoting various ministries. We stopped by a display for Toccoa Falls College and Graduate School. I spoke to the representative and asked, "Do you offer any courses in counseling?" He described their program to me and then said, "Why don't you consider going through the Master's Degree Program in Pastoral Studies?" Now having graduated college twenty-fours years before, I was not quite sure how to answer that question. After all, I just wanted to get information on one or two courses, and maybe just audit them anyway. Sounded like a pretty monumental commitment to me. Joanie and I talked about it and found our district superintendent and asked him to give us a recommendation. We brought this information back to the representative and applied right there during that council.

I was accepted in the graduate degree program and enrolled the following fall. Joanie and I decided to trust God to supply the financial need, time to go to school, and the ability to do the work. I am so grateful to the churches and individuals who helped me along the way financially, with their prayers, and with their encouragement.

I still remember my first course in the graduate program at Toccoa Falls College. I had not done any formal study since my undergraduate work at Nyack College, which was completed in 1973. To say that I was feeling some apprehension was putting it mildly. But in a very short time, I discovered I was in the company of a number of students who were at the same stage in life as myself. As a result, I became excited, and I accepted the challenge of being stretched by God to learn how to more effectively serve Him and His Church even after twenty-four years in the ministry.

I was forty-six years old at the time and had a goal to graduate by the age of fifty. By God's grace that was accomplished in the summer of 2001. I found the interaction with my fellow students and the personal approach of the professors to be most refreshing. It was wonderful to watch God provide for this education both financially and by giving me an increased desire to learn more about ministry in our changing culture.

The modular format (a concentrated, twenty-seven-hour week) allowed me to maintain the ministry responsibilities while balancing my responsibilities as a husband and father.

I also found time on campus (what time there was after living at the library), to be a refreshing break from the demands of ministry. I grew during each of those weeks away as I developed new friendships and enjoyed my time with my Lord. I developed new tools for ministry, made some new lifetime friends, and have gained new insights into my own heart regarding my personal call to ministry. What have I gained from those years? To be open to God's direction, trust Him completely to supply my needs, maintain a teachable spirit, and to anticipate His blessing on my life.

After four years, about 17,000 miles of driving and $10,000 of God's provision, I received my master's degree in pastoral studies. About half way through the program, I wrote the following journal entry:

> I only know that in every city the Holy Spirit warns me that prison and hardships are facing me. However, I consider my life worth nothing to me; if only I may finish the race and complete the task the Lord Jesus has given me—the task of testifying to the gospel of God's grace.
> (Acts 20:23-24)

Then, I wrote a phrase that I have said to Him often: "God I depend on You to enable me to finish well!"

Near the end of my program in April of 2001 I wrote:

> Made a fresh commitment today to have regular times of silence and solitude! How can I hear from God with so much noise going on around me? Lord, I must pray, commune, listen and be still before You all through the day! I love You, my Lord!

During the week of my final course I wrote:

> Woke up at 5:30 am—Great awareness of sin and my own wicked heart, at times! Repented of TV watching as a waste of time and cried tears of brokenness in my bed, and then I was drawn to the close, sweet presence of God again. I cried tears of joy for forgiveness and God's love

washed over me! I love You, my God! Keep me clean and pure for Yourself. You are coming soon!

I remember that morning. God was so close, right there in the middle of my brokenness. He is so real. Then on the last day of class I wrote: "Lord, thank You for this day of completion of graduate school (four years). You are awesome and great! Thanks for expanding my heart and life! I love You!

God used going back to school to do many things in my life. As I now reflect on those days, I have come to believe that the main reason for me to go back to school was to learn the value of spiritual disciplines and to grow more in love with my Lord. Both of those areas continue to grow in my life, and I praise God for His ongoing presence and direction.

Throughout the years of restoring our lives, I, Joan, have found that the goodness of God knows no end and His mercies are truly new every morning. His provision for us has been sufficient and satisfying. Walking hand in hand with God is to know the complete meaning of oneness with Him. Learning to totally depend on Him for my every need is teaching me the depth of His love for me. His love is absolutely limitless. Truly, if God be for me, who can be against me! So, when my husband decided to go for his master's degree, I was very supportive of this opportunity. I knew this would be good for him and his ministry in the church.

When he started to take the classes, our oldest child, Dan had gone to college and our other two children were in high school. By the time Dad's graduation came around, all our children had graduated high school and were making plans for their own lives.

There were many changes during the years of his studies. I would travel with him when he would go to Toccoa, Georgia, and he would drop me off to visit family. As Bobby would prepare to go to college to study, I would stay with my children who lived in Gainesville, or I would go to Atlanta and stay with my parents. It would be an opportunity for me to travel with him, and then I would have special visits with my grandchildren. It was not always easy to travel all those miles, but it was worth it in the end. When Dad graduated, we were all so proud of him and threw him a party to celebrate his accomplishment.

Before the clarity of God's new call would be revealed to us, it would be preceded by summer struggles.

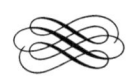

Chapter 12

Summer Struggles

Throughout the summer of 2000, I was going through a period of restlessness. As I was finishing my course work at graduate school, I was sensing that I would be going through another transition in my life. However, this time would be unlike any other transition I had ever known. The best way I can describe this to you is that you believe something is about to happen in your life, but that is all you know for the moment.

I was having a greater passion for the entire world. I was looking to make a difference in the lives of others who could make a difference. One day I received in the mail a recruiting brochure for the chaplaincy program in the army. Normally I would put this in "file 13." But that day I read it with great interest. I even sent away for videotape explaining the program. I called Joanie on the phone, fully expecting her to blow this off. I know how difficult it was for her to relocate from place to place throughout our ministry together.

To my surprise she was not against the idea and actually encouraged me to pursue it. My jaw almost fell to the floor as I heard her voice on the other end of the phone filled with enthusiasm and anticipation.

I contacted a recruiter and found out that I was too old and did not have enough hours in my master's degree program to meet their requirements. The reason I share this story with you is to demonstrate that something very different and new was happening within both of us at the same time. As we talked later that evening, we were both having a larger vision for ministry, both geographically and numerically, than we had ever had previously. We did not quite know what this meant except that we were on the same page and would begin to seek God for His specific direction for the days ahead.

When I called my son David, who serves our country in the United States Air Force, he laughed without stopping. He could not imagine his dad in the service. There is nothing like your children to keep you humble. I was able to laugh with him as we enjoyed the moment and let it go.

But there was a deeper issue that would not go away. Every time I looked at a world map, it took on a new meaning for me. I began to take a personal interest in various parts of the world. I would place my hands on maps in my home (recently put up about that time) and pray over the world. My prayers were changing toward the entire world and that was happening more often as this passion grew greater. In mid-August I wrote in my journal: "Be steadfast, immovable, always abounding in the work of the Lord, knowing that your labor is not in vain in the Lord" (1 Corinthians 15:58). I understood that what we do for God counts for eternity. I wrote: "Work done for God endures long after the worker dies.

Summer Struggles

About the same time, I was reading and meditating about living a life of simplicity. Joanie and I usually lived a fairly simple lifestyle, but we had both agreed to scale down where we could and not take on any debt. We had a desire to be debt free so that we could go anywhere God would lead us without the care of any obligations.

This is so foreign to the thinking of the average American, especially during those days of easy credit, many unsolicited credit card applications filling our mailboxes, and the very popular "buy now pay later" way of life that many people subscribe to.

The fun part about this is that we were actually enjoying this mindset and both wanted to be entirely free to serve God wherever, to whomever, and whenever. When I was younger, I was consumed with owning things. We never had much, but I at least wanted whatever it was to be mine. I have learned in recent years that while enjoying things, I don't want to be consumed with owning them. I am not advocating this for anyone else; this was our own preparation for what was to be God's new call on our lives in the days to follow.

During the end of that summer, I was reading and quite taken up with a book written by Reggie McNeal. He writes:

> No one can calculate how many would-be leaders go down into the wilderness. The leader cannot advance to the next level without passing the entrance exam—the call clarification. The leader cannot emerge from the wilderness until this challenge is met. God is patient in the wilderness. He uses the experience to sculpt the leader's heart. We see the wilderness as something to avoid or to spend as little time in as possible. Ask Moses about spending forty years there. We expect God to pave for us

a road to public acclaim. Ask David about being driven into the outback. We believe academic training will route us around the wilderness and graduate us into ministry leadership. Ask Paul about the school of the desert. Some of the wilderness testing will show the face of the devil. Ask Jesus. This remains a profound mystery. God uses wilderness trials, even the devil's wiles, as tools in his heart surgery.[1]

That was where I was, and God was preparing me for an entirely new adventure with Him. I knew that we were on the verge of a new way of thinking, trusting, living, and ministering. God knew exactly what He was doing, and what God does He does well.

As I, Joan, think back over these last months, I cannot believe how much has happened to bring me where I am today. The day my husband called about getting in touch with the United States Army to find out about being a chaplain, I was sitting at the computer looking at our mail. As he shared his idea, my heart leaped inside me and I said "Yes, let's go!" I thought to myself as I hung up the phone that maybe this is what God was moving on my heart when I had this desire to be a part of something big. "Something" that would allow us to share Christ in a big way. It was nebulous, just a feeling, something hard to put into words, but it left me with a hunger to do something big for God. This had to be it.

Then my chair became my altar as my heart poured out to God. I know the Holy Spirit fell on me. His presence and love were so real. I prayed and raised my hands and told God that I would go anywhere with Him. I let go of all my little, earthly possessions, my house, our car, furniture; I would by His enabling leave it all for Him. I love Him and I want to go where He leads.

The hard part came as I thought of my children and the very strong pull they have on my heart because I love them and my grandchildren. This was much harder and tears came coursing down my cheeks. I sobbed with the reality of giving up my children and their children. In my heart, I gave them to the Lord and held nothing back. I just knew I would never see them again because God would ask me to go to some far-off place where I couldn't see them.

I love my children with all my heart, and I am so proud of them. It is hard enough that I don't get to see them because of the distance. In my heart as I prayed, I was saying good-bye as if I would not see them anymore. Now there was nothing holding me back. All my children were on their own and it is just my husband and me.

Once again I was about to find out just what kind of awesome God I had decided to love with all my heart. I honestly thought that I would not live near my children and that God would immediately take us far away for ministry, but that is not what has happened.

God has allowed me to have some very close, personal time with my adult children, and their children, and my son who is in the United States Air Force. I am so grateful and so loved by our wonderful God. He is so good to me. I never expected Him to let me live near my children, but He did. I know that it will not be for long, but that is fine with me. God has lovingly given me such a special time with my grandchildren and my adult children that I am too happy and will treasure it in my heart for years to come. Thank You so much, dear God.

I want to take you back with me to look at another time in my life where God spoke to my heart. I want you to see what I believe is God's hand showing up in similar ways as He is weaving the tapestry of my life. I can remember a time when I had this thought run through my mind, *Do I want to get closer to God or not?* It was as if something monumental was about to happen by my response to this question. I had to make a very important decision. I remember asking myself, *Do you want to be what people call a fanatic?* I couldn't get the question out of my mind. Did I want to be closer to God? The question weighed heavily on my mind. What I would decide seemed like it would change my life. I think of it as a turning point in my life. I decided in my heart that I would get closer to God. I would do whatever it took to know Him better and serve Him completely. This was a very quiet and firm decision. I made this commitment in my heart by myself, and I really did not tell anyone about it. I wasn't in a church service or at an altar. I was in my routines of life, cleaning the kitchen and caring for my children.

I know now that it was the Holy Spirit drawing me closer to God as in Jeremiah 31:3, "I have loved you with an everlasting love; I have drawn you with lovingkindness." I understand more than ever that Jesus is a relationship. I accepted Christ as my Savior around the age of six and grew up in a Christian home. I know that God desires to be intimate with every one of His creations. He is a very personal God. He is very alive and active, always pursuing, calling, looking, and drawing His children into an intimate, personal walk with Him.

Lately, He has called again and asked me if I would follow Him deeper still. Would I fully surrender my life to Him? How did this thought come to me? Once again, by a thought in my mind that said, *I am tired of finding myself striving to live in closeness to God and keep joyful.*

I was falling back into my old ways of trying to please God. I didn't want to go down that road again. I know where striving ends up. In this conversation with God, I said, "I want You in my life more than anything, but I am tired of trying to live the way You ask. I *give up*. I can't do it anymore. You have to do it. Either You are the God You say You are, or You are not. I am not going to try to live this life anymore. I can't do it!"

Then, as I sat there in my living room, I felt a peace come over me (and I wasn't even looking for any kind of response). With tears of gratitude, I lifted up my hand and said, "God, I love You, and I want to follow You. I give You my hand."

I closed my hand as a child would put her hand into her father's. It was as if God clasped my hand in His. I said, "This is how I will follow You with my hand in yours. I surrender. I give up trying to control my life. I will never take my hand out of yours for the rest of my life, and I know You will never let go of mine. Thank You, my Father God." Having made this meaningful commitment, I was content that if God wanted me to sit in my living room for the rest of my life (so to speak), I would. I really never expected what was to happen next. I only desired to be closer to God.

Our wonderful God wants all His children close to His heart and moving on in our adventure with Him. He desires all His creation to commune with Him. Remember how God would come in the cool of the evening to walk and talk with Adam and Eve? He hasn't changed, He still desires to walk and talk with all His children if we will only listen for His still, small voice. He is calling to your heart, too. Won't you let Him in? You may have to struggle to get to the point where you are willing, but it will be worth it. The struggle leads you to God, and He will never let you down. You will, like me, find out that He is who He says

He is. When I showed God my heart was willing to let Him be in control, He began to show my husband and me His new call for us.

Chapter 13
God's New Call

It was a Sunday afternoon about 2:00 PM. I was in a chapel service along with other men from a prison ministry and about thirty inmates from a correctional institution. It was a maximum-security prison where we spent four days sharing God's love and then went back on a monthly basis to encourage and build friendships in the Lord.

The date was August 26, 2001. That date will be forever fixed in my mind and in my heart. Why? This was the time when God's new call began to be placed on my heart. I invite you now to take a trip with me back to that day.

We lined up at the gate as usual, went through our security checks, greeted one another, and then went inside the prison and made our way to the chapel. There were about fifty of us between our prison ministry team members and those who were incarcerated. This had become a ministry that had a very special place in my heart.

As we took our seats and began to share with each other, we soon were led into a time of singing praises to God. This was all very familiar and very wonderful. When we sang, I was deeply touched by the Spirit of God.

As I, along with my brothers, was singing, the presence of God came over me, and, as clear as day, He spoke to my heart in His still, small voice. I was still and weeping as I know God said to my heart: "I will lead you into something totally new, unlike anything you have ever done before. I will lead you. Trust in Me alone!"

I did not know what to make of this. I just knew it was my Lord because His impressions on my heart were similar to other occasions when He spoke to me. As I left the prison gates that afternoon, I would wait for God's plan to be revealed. I knew beyond any shadow of a doubt that something very different and marvelous would be taking place that only God could do.

Joanie and I agreed to begin a new journal, recording how God would speak to us through His Word and prayer in the days to come regarding a new ministry. The following Sunday, I was aware of the power of God in the service. I was told by a friend, "The whole world is your ministry." I began to get a greater burden for the world and the need for repentance, healing, and restoration. I believed that both Joanie and I would be led into a new calling for God.

I wrote the following journal entry dated 9/15/2001:

> Joanie went for her first training session as a counselor in a new ministry she was involved in, and after she left I walked back and forth in the living room and prayed asking God to speak to my heart regarding the future ministry. He spoke to my heart and revealed to me that He would lead us, and He would be our Source and Supply. We were not to look to men but receive things from His Hand. Then the geography of England, the Czech

Republic, Russia, and Italy came to my heart. . . It was a special time of prayer.

In the days to follow, I would wake up hours earlier than usual and ask God for His direction, read His Word, and lay myself out before His Presence. This continued for about a month as He met me in very deep and personal ways. When we are serious about hearing from God, He will speak to us. I would often weep, go through periods of brokenness, receive His blessed peace, and then enter into wonderful times of prayer and adoration to my Lord. I became very specific in my prayers and knew God was moving mightily in my heart.

All during this time, I continued my pastoral ministry and prison ministry as well. Although the road ahead of me was not yet known, I had a strong sense of God's direction to be quiet and stay before Him and trust Him to continue what He began in my heart.

God's peace was very real during that time. Joanie and I entered into new territory as we felt led to ask people who came in our home or when we were in the homes of others to pray over them. Several times the waves of God's Presence was evident as each of us wept before Him with thanksgiving and brokenness that He would use us in that way.

Things were no longer as they used to be regarding our comings and goings. We found ourselves stopping along the way and praying about everything. God was moving in great ways, and we did not want to miss anything. We purchased a map of the United States and another map of the world. We also got a detailed map of Europe and put these all over the walls of our study. Many times I would go and place my hands over countries and the entire world on these maps and weep and pray to God. I had never had such a worldwide burden as this in my life.

Throughout the month of October 2001, I recorded some very specific things God was establishing in my heart. These would prove to be pivotal transitions in the coming months.

10/14/2002:
Very heavy time in the Word while preaching from Habakkuk. 3:1,2. The congregation's open response to repentance and prayer was most moving. God called me to lay hands and pray over two young men for future ministry. He is moving mightily. Went back to the prison ministry after the service.
As I quietly left the service to return to the prison ministry, people were still praying out loud, confessing in brokenness to God. His Presence was awesome! I wept with tears of joy and sorrow as I drove away.

10/15/2001:
Shared with the leadership of the church that I do not believe that I would be the pastor of another church in the future. I desire to continue on here until God leads me out.

10/16/2001:
Spent four hours with Joanie regarding this call to ministry as we both ended up on our knees before God for His direction and giving Him our availability.

10/16-20/2001:
The call of pastor is being lifted from me and an overwhelming call to be an evangelist; a tool of God for repentance and restoration came over my heart. I am asking God for miracles and healings as a testimony to the awesome power of God and a way to point people to Jesus and as an encouragement for the believers. Felt the

need to put together a prayer support team and began making contacts.

God is using Joanie in her counseling ministry and a new spirit of boldness and purpose is coming over her. Praise God for His calling on our lives. We have committed afresh to pray more *together*.

In prayer, Australia was added to my heart as a place of ministry. Began to seek God for a name for this ministry for the glory of God. Woke up early this morning for prayer for the world. This morning I laid my hands on a map of the world and wept. God is increasing this vision and burden on both our hearts. He said over and over that He would let us know *soon!*

Now when I say that I woke up early in the morning, my usual wake up time is about 5:30 AM. For several weeks I was up between 2:30-4:00 AM, and although I was very tired, the Presence of God was so wonderful that I looked forward to those mornings. This pattern ended after about four to five weeks, and I got some much-needed rest.

Why have I given you so much personal detail? Because the purpose of the book is to demonstrate how God wants intimacy with His people and when we seek Him, He will be found. This closeness is for all who will come to Him. Your story will be different, but our God is the same. Seek Him with all of your heart. He is longing for you.

As a matter of fact, this morning (5/31/2002), I woke up at about 3:00 AM and after my time with God, felt the strong urge to continue to write this chapter. The last two hours have been wonderful as I recount God's goodness and faithful direction.

Whatever God chooses to do in *your life*, when He prompts you, go for it! You will be blessed and He will be glorified!

During the fall of 2001, God continued to speak clearly through His Word regarding some things that Joanie and I would need to be prepared for and equipped with for the coming days of God's new call on our lives. I would invite you to have a seat, get a cup of coffee and your Bible, and take a look at a few more of my journal entries and ask God what He might say to your own heart.

10/25/2001:
This morning we (Joanie and I) were searching for the Scripture that spoke about God giving us words when we needed them. Luke 12:11-12 states: "And when you are brought to trial in the synagogues and before rulers and authorities, don't worry about what to say in your defense, for the Holy Spirit will teach you what needs to be said even as you are standing there." This will be such a necessity when the day comes that we are called upon to stand up for God regardless of what the cost may be. God is our Rock, Strong Tower, Defender, and Jesus is our Advocate. Praise His holy name.

10/26/2001:
God blessed me this morning with 2 Kings 4:1-7. This Scripture tells the story of Elisha and the widow's oil. Verse 6: "When all the jars were full, she said to her son, 'Bring me another one.' But he replied, 'There is not a jar left.' Then the oil stopped flowing." The number of the jars gathered was an indication of the faith. God's provision was as large as their faith and willingness to obey. We must not limit God's blessing by our lack of faith and obedience. See Ephesians 3:20-21: "Now to him who is able to do immeasurably more than we ask or imagine, according to his power that is at work within us, to him be glory in the church and in Christ Jesus throughout all generations, forever and ever! Amen.

I trust God for miracles, healings, and a large response to the preaching of the Word in the days to come for His glory and the salvation and restoration of many for the Kingdom of God.

It was becoming clear to me that my trust must be in God Alone! He would prepare me for difficult days ahead. His provision financially, with opportunities to minister, building a ministry team, prayer partners, and other needs would be directed and met by God Himself. Now the question for me to consider would be this one: Would I trust God completely for all things? You see it is one thing to discuss faith but quite another thing to live by faith.

God would take me through another one of His "schools" in this new area of my life. I would come to realize that this was not man's work nor would God bless man's efforts. I had been there and done that and never wanted to return to those ways of ministry. As God's new call was being birthed in my heart, I would now need to commit to a new level of trust and dependency on Him alone. I believe that is what the Bible calls faith.

God was moving mightily on our hearts in order to establish our new call from Him. My husband mentioned my opportunity to be involved in a ministry in my community. As my heart was being moved toward God and as He was revealing Himself to me, I felt a desire to reach out of my comfort zone and do something tangible with my new commitments.

Through my church, I became aware of a ministry to women in our community and made an appointment with the director to find out what I could do there. I had told God that I would become involved in this ministry if I had a car to get there. A couple weeks later, a friend called and offered me a car for several months. I thanked God, called the director, and began a regular commitment every week to counsel women.

This commitment was very stretching for me, and God used it to fill my heart with love and compassion for hurting women. I learned to allow the Holy Spirit to lead me in an area of my life where I felt very inadequate, and to put it honestly, scared to be involved.

He showed me that He would lead me and give me the words to share. I found the ability to listen, share, and pray as the situations allowed, and the Holy Spirit guided me. I made this entry in my diary one day:

> God is calling my heart into an adventure. I think it has to do with these end times as we draw closer to the return of our Lord, and I will answer the call. I think this community ministry is my training, my classroom. I believe God is moving on my heart and asking me to go with Him to a deeper level of commitment and a higher level of living than I have before. I know the Holy Spirit is helping me to live in Jesus and helping me to become sensitive to what God wants to do. My heart desires to abandon myself into God, to be ready to go where He leads me, and to do what He gives me to do at a moment's notice. I am letting my heart go and learning to listen to His voice and obey Him. I want to do this. I love God. I hope I will pass the test. I believe I will because God said what He has begun He will accomplish and I *know* I can count on Him.

I wish I could say that all my lessons and new belief systems were so totally in place that I didn't struggle anymore with anything God would ask me to do, but that is not the case. I can say that God is faithful, and every time I have an objection to what He is asking me to do, He gives me the encouragement I need.

An example of His word to me is recorded in my diary, "God my Father said this to my heart—I love you. I am always with you. I will be there for you when you jump off the cliff; in fact we will jump off the cliff together!" This word gave me strength and confidence when I shared a teaching in front of the church or went to the women's ministry. It will continue to serve me as a reminder of God's presence with me whenever I do something He asks. Every objection I brought Him along the way about fulfilling His new call for us, He has answered.

Another word from Him settled my questions concerning my education. I wrote in my diary:

> Today as I prayed, I broke down and cried for God overwhelmed me with His goodness, power, and love for me. He put His finger on a weak spot in my life—my feeling of inadequacy in having only two years of college. Before I could finish my objection, He stopped me and impressed on my heart that it would be He—His anointing, His power, His wisdom—that would fit me for His use.

I am reminded of 2 Corinthians 4:7, "But we have this treasure in jars of clay to show that this all-surpassing power is from God and not from us." Education is good and God may use it to equip me, but He is not limited by my lack of four years of college. On another day, I made this entry in my diary,

> "Just make yourself available to me," God spoke to my heart. I read in Acts 4:13 where Peter and John had no

special training and the thought struck me that they were fisherman—and I am a mother and wife—God will use me, too.

Shortly after, I wrote this response in my diary,

> I prayed Mary's prayer to God in Luke 1:38, "I am the Lord's servant. May it be to me as you have said." This is my answer to God for putting His hand on me and asking me to let the Holy Spirit lead my life and use me. Thank You, God.

During these days, I was amazed at how much God was moving and speaking to me. I normally did not live this way. I wanted to hear everything. God was dealing with my heart and testing me in small, everyday ways to see if I meant what I had said. The words we say and the things we commit to will be tested.

I was coming home from having a haircut, and my hairdresser did not take my money that day. She wanted me to be encouraged and keep it. As I was on my way home, I stopped at the post office to get our mail. It was Christmas time, so there was a person by the door collecting money for the needy. I was passing by and heard my thought say, *Put the money in the bucket.*

I kept walking to my mailbox and after I got my mail I tried to question if this was the Holy Spirit because I didn't want to just give my money away. I wasn't even able to finish the question because the impression in my heart was so clear and strong. I placed the money in the bucket and felt such joy. As I left, it was as if God said to me that He wanted me to get used to listening and obeying Him.

I learned much about the connection of our heart with our life in God. Suddenly, so much of my life up to this point came into sharper focus for me. God has been taking me on my adventure with Him, the adventure that He put together for me since before I was born. He has been taking me along by the hand or carrying me when necessary to get me there. He has been calling my heart all along even using my breakdown to get my heart in a place where I would hear Him clearly call me. He has orchestrated this whole thing, and it causes me to say, "Thank You, Lord. Nothing is lost in the hard places of my life. You have redeemed it all."

He made me ready to hear Him ask me to follow Him and to desire to abandon myself into His love. "Yes, Lord, I want to let it all go and follow You. You have plans and purposes for me, and I want to fulfill them. I want to go where You are." God will take me at the very place in my life where I finally surrender, stop trying to call my own shots and say "Yes, Lord, You take control of me – You tell me where to go and what to say." I have decided to align myself to His will—to His plans and purposes for me so that I may follow Him. In my heart—in the deepest parts of my being, I pledge allegiance to the Lamb, my Lord and Savior Jesus Christ, and desire His life to be glorified in me. I pledge my life to Him—no matter where it takes me, for I am safest in His will.

I desire to abandon my life into His hands and live with Him in surrender—without concern of the consequences which is reckless abandon because I have placed myself in His hands and He is responsible to keep me. I will follow where His Spirit leads me believing that He will equip me and protect me as I listen to His voice. He is my provision and I have no need that He cannot fulfill. Jesus Christ is my example and He came to earth to show me how to live this life of reckless abandon. He placed Himself in the care of the heavenly Father and was completely reliant upon Him for every word He spoke and every move He made. I desire that my heart be so captivated by His love that nothing else but pleasing Him and loving Him will matter to me.

I am excited that this wonderful God wants our hearts, and He desires that we throw ourselves into His hand and not worry about what will happen to us. I am sick and tired of worrying about is going to happen to me. That is not my responsibility—that is His responsibility. I would rather put my energy into listening for His voice and following where He leads. I want to let other people know that there is an awesome God that totally loves them and has a marvelous plan for their lives.

He also has the means to see that you and I live that marvelous plan. We have to do the hard part—give up, let Him be in control, and walk by faith, not by sight. I say, yes, by the power and love of the Holy Spirit, we can do it!

In my reading, I came across a thought that stood out to me concerning Hebrews 12:1 and I would like to share with you. It goes something like this—when we come to our crossroads, when we have to make a very important decision, will we press on in our walk with God or will we turn around and go back in defeat? It is as if the cloud of witnesses is watching, holding their breath in anticipation of what our decision will be. When we go on they cheer us with great joy and anticipation! I love the picture this paints for me. It thrills me to think the saints who have gone on before us are cheering us on in our walk with God, hoping we will decide to go deeper with reckless abandon into our walk with Almighty God.

My husband and I were about to take a leap of faith as we continued our ongoing adventure with God.

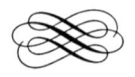

Chapter 14
A Leap of Faith

"Now faith is being sure of what we hope for and certain of what we do not see" (Hebrews 11:1). One day I did a short word study of this Scripture to get a fuller understanding of its implication. I discovered: "Now faith (proof, a pledge—to persuade, to have confidence) is being sure (substance, support) of what we hope (expected, anticipated) for, and certain (evidence, a proof, test) of what we do not see."

Could I grow into a place in my life where I would trust God beyond my wildest dreams? That was becoming my desire as this implicit trust in God would be necessary for the new ministry He would entrust to us. I would have to be utterly convinced that all that God says is true. Could I place the care of my family under His care, when for so many years I had been the provider? Could I be still enough to hear His voice, when so often I was so busy listening to my own? Could He in fact lead Joanie and me from place to place as we fully put ourselves at His disposal? This new level of trust and commitment would bring us both into a life of complete abandonment before our Lord.

If something is true, then it will be worthy of our trust. God's Word is true. Therefore God can be trusted. "For the word of the Lord is right and true; he is faithful in all he does" (Psalm 33:4). Throughout the entire Word of God and the course of history, the testimony of God has proven to be true. His Word stands forever. This is the One I choose to place my complete confidence and trust in forever. A true faith in God would lead Joanie and me into a new dimension of living founded entirely on our persuasion that He would do what He promised to do. Now it would become our responsibility and high privilege to believe God and act on that belief.

Throughout the fall of 2001, over and over again I knew the Lord was preparing Joanie and me for a new walk of faith. He continued to speak to my heart and assure me that He would take care of us and we were to trust in Him alone. We were beginning to have our faith tested as the usual ways our needs were met changed to a total dependence on God. God's faithfulness can be trusted. I remember reading or hearing the following statement: "When we can't see God's hand, we can trust His heart."

Since we knew God and were loved by Him, we did not have to have everything clearly revealed to us in advance. I am learning first hand the reality of another truth that I remember reading somewhere: "You don't need to know where you are going, if you know whom you are following." I like that very much. I believe that entirely.

Joanie and I have staked our entire future on the faithfulness of God. We know Whom we are following. It is certainly up to God to direct us in His time and in His way regarding where we are going. Although Joanie and I knew all these principles, we discussed at length and sought the

A Leap of Faith

Lord in prayer often regarding a decision as important as this one. We did not want to miss what God had for us while at the same time this total, uncompromising faith in God alone would stretch us beyond any past experiences and into a new level of trust on our Lord. We shared openly about such a decision and recognized that others may not understand this or give their blessing, but was it not God who was doing the calling? Would it not be God in Whom we would invest our lives, and therefore, could we not place our every need before Him? To take such a leap of faith would not be a blind leap as the capable Arms of God Himself would be our security and provision. Joanie and I were in the process of trusting our future, with all of its uncertainties to God who knows all things.

As we began to investigate the procedure for incorporating the new ministry, the following journal entry was dated 11/26/2001:

> As we met with a wonderful Christian lawyer today, he asked us to share our vision for the new ministry. As we were applying for incorporation, I asked him how much his fee would be, and his response was, "There is none." I then asked him what the value of his service would be and he said, "That is not your concern. You have more important things to do." I wept and we prayed over him and his office. God is good.

God was beginning to bring people along our path that would be favorable to this ministry and help us along the way. This would be one of several of God's provisions for our needs.

I believe that God was now calling me to be "sold out" to Him as never before. This would be a love relationship with my Lord and Savior Jesus Christ that was worth more to me than *anything* else in the world. I wrote the following journal entry dated 11/30/2001:

> 2 Corinthians 8:2-3 states, "Though they had been going through much trouble and hard times [The Macedonians], their wonderful joy and deep poverty have overflowed in rich generosity. For I can testify that they gave not only what they could afford but far more. And they did it of their own free will." I pray Lord that these Scriptures will be lived out in the ministry days to come wherever and to whomever You lead us. I have just spent the last two-and-a-half hours with my wonderful Lord. I am realizing in a new way the depth of His love for me. Praise His holy Name!

Have you ever come across something in your reading that keeps coming back to you? It is like a treasure that when unearthed continues to enrich your life repeatedly. Each time you read this gem and meditate on its truth, you get thoroughly blessed all over again as the wonderful truth of your discovery is practically fleshed out in your life.

During my course work in graduate school I came upon such a treasure that I would like to share with you. It comes from the pen of Warren Wiersbe:

> Just be sure that your preaching is an act of worship, and that you prepare each message and each service so as to "proclaim the praises of Him who called you out of darkness into His marvelous light" (1 Peter 2:9). Keep in mind that the harvest is not the end of the meeting: it's the end of the age. Minister by faith. God promises to do the rest."[1]

That has come back to me more times than I can count. This has freed me from the previous burden to be result oriented. My responsibility is to proclaim God's Truth by faith. That's it! It is not my concern to place time expectations or physical manifestations related to any response to His Word. Wow! Is that wonderful truth? I am living under an entirely new freedom in the proclamation of the gospel. I am realizing more and more every day that it is all up to God. The response after the message is God's concern. My place is to simply and truthfully deliver the "mail' intended for the reader. The Author of the love letter (God's Word) is responsible to quicken the heart of the reader. Now that is freedom and provides me with great joy as I rest securely in God's Sovereignty to bring to pass His desired purposes. The harvest is God's responsibility. The timing and response of men's hearts are His business. The faith to trust in His Power and His Word doing all that He intended it to do is my responsibility. I can hardly contain myself in sharing with you the truth just stated. The transformation that the belief and practice of this truth has made in my personal life and ministry has and continues to be glorious.

I believe that many believers today do not walk in faith and liberty (as I did not years ago), because they do not see the greatness of God. When we come to understand that He truly loves us intimately and desires for us to live above what we have settled for so often, we can abandon ourselves completely to Him. There is no alternative for the child of God who is sold out to His plans and purposes for their lives. Why? Because the One who created us and has wonderful things in store for us, waits for us to be completely stripped of ourselves so that He then can use us (Galatians 2:20).

The great news along the way is that God never removes something from us without pouring back into us far more than we ever gave up. I am convinced that greater than any gift or ability that He bestows on us is His friendship, intimacy, and heart for us. Stop and think on that before reading any more in this chapter. I have prayed during the writing of these words the Holy Spirit of God would flood you with His love, grace, kindness, peace, forgiveness, and mercy.

You see God wants your *heart,* and upon having your heart, He will have all of you. How much of your heart does He truly have? The answer to that question will have a direct bearing on your walk with Him, your trust of Him, and your motive for service to Him. My prayer for you is that you will be deeply moved as God's Spirit yearns for your heart to be captured by His love, and when that happens, you too will never be the same!

As I read from the pen and heart of Brennan Manning during my early hours with God one morning, I found myself connecting with where my commitment was heading.

> Reckless confidence for me is the unshakable conviction that Jesus and the Father love me in a way that defies imagination. It means to accept without reservation all the Abba of Jesus has ordained for my life... Perhaps the only honest measure of the recklessness of my confidence is my readiness for martyrdom. Not only my willingness to die for Him and the sake of the Gospel, but to live for Him one day at a time.[2]

Whatever God allows in my life for His glory, as I abandon myself to Him, I minister to whomever, wherever, and whenever He leads me. I gave up my rights long ago to the One who rightfully owns me. I love God so much that all that matters to me is what He wants, and that becomes revealed to me as He has more and more of my heart. There is no better way to live than totally immersing ourselves into a deep, intimate, growing love relationship with God. This commitment brings a price, but many of us have paid a great price seeking that which brings no real joy—following the wrong leaders, relying on ourselves and others, etc. Isn't about time to really live for God?

During this time in our journey (November-December, 2001), Joanie and I were praying and counting the cost of living a life totally submitted to God for His glory. We were consumed with His Presence, in awe of His Power, counting on His Provision, being led according to His Purpose, and in love with His Person!

It has been said that God works in mysterious ways, His wonders to perform. His ways are mysterious because they are different from what we would do. As Isaiah 55:8 says, "For my thoughts are not your thoughts, neither are your ways my ways." I, Joan, think that statement is so true. What a blessing it has been in my life.

I love when I can see the hand of God at work in my husband and me. God has always worked that way in our marriage by moving on both our hearts when He calls us into new areas of ministry. This time was no different. He placed this new call on both our hearts.

In the beginning, God revealed the changes that would be coming to my husband. As Bob would share these changes with me, God would confirm it in my heart. As we placed ourselves in His hands and obeyed the directions He gave us, I began to ask the Holy Spirit to show me for myself how He specifically wanted me involved in this new ministry. This is how together my husband and I were able to take this leap of faith.

As I continued to grow into this new calling along with my husband, I began asking God to change me from the inside out. What do I mean by this? I needed to hear from God myself and not only receive my direction through my husband. Up to this point in our lives and ministry, I had received my direction (where we would live, what church we would attend) through my husband. As I read Scripture and understand the way God works between husband and wives, this is totally normal and has only deepened.

Now, I began to hear God speaking into my heart and confirming in me that He was bringing me into my own ministry right alongside my husband. I knew I was called to bring the message of Jesus to the world and have a ministry of love and encouragement to people as well as my husband. God began to reveal this calling on my own heart and life separately as well as together with my husband.

This is awesome for me. It has filled a void in my heart, giving me a purpose now that my children were grown up with families of their own. When God placed this call on my heart, I realized the fears and hesitations I felt would have to be dealt with in order for me to abandon myself into His adventure for me.

I can truly say that God has been a very thorough and loving teacher. He helped me to see that I had some more inner work to do in order for Him to heal me and free me from my fears. He showed me that I must place myself into His hands and go deeper into trusting Him as a child would trust her father. I must let go of past struggles and place my hurts and disappointments into His Father heart of love for me and let Him heal my inner child. I must trust Him to be there for me.

As I realized these truths, I have decided to believe my Father God. He has assured me that when I go forward to do a work for Him, He will be there with me. I will not be alone. I will be surrounded and indwelt by Him. Only what He permits will happen in my life.

He is for me, and with Him on my side I have nothing to fear. Psalm 46:2 says, "Therefore we will not fear, though the earth give way and the mountains fall into the heart of the sea." He will be there for me. I am established in His care. I believe that even in the midst of turmoil and trouble, if I am where God wants me to be, I am in the safest place in the world. No harm can befall me for I am covered by His hand. It is like being in the eye of the storm where all is peaceful and calm even though all around is stormy and violent.

It is totally His responsibility to take care of me. I am safe. I believe that this Father God who made the heavens and the earth, who parted the Red Sea for His beloved Israel, who raised Lazarus from the dead, and felled the walls of Jericho for His children will be there for me. I can trust Him because He is my Father and He loves me.

God knew I needed this inner assurance, and He has given this to me to enable me to go forward, to help me to get out of the boat and stop trying to be safe inside my little world. Now I can, by His power and love for me, minister His Word and testify with assurance that this Father God is who He says He is. God is awesome.

A few years ago, God gave me this poem, and I put it in writing to glorify His name and His awesome love. It is for all of us. I would like to share it with you:

> Jesus Christ came down from heaven to earth,
>   To give, to love, to die.
>   Freely. Unconditionally.
>
> He holds His arms open to me. "Receive what I am
>   giving," He says, "to live in fullness of joy."
> He lays it all - forgiveness of sins, newness of life - at my
>   disposal—

But will I make it mine and accept His free gift of unconditional love, or will I turn my back on Him and not live in victory?

Did He suffer and die in vain? Of course not!

But if I choose to say "No" and refuse to accept His gift of love then it is like I am saying it does not matter that He died for me - For rejection is death and pain.

He stands at the door of my life offering me total love and acceptance in spite of my sin.

Oh, what a Savior! Oh, what a King! Glorious, God, Almighty. Holiness.
Righteousness is my King.

Did He suffer and die in vain? Of course not!
His suffering and death brought me life and joy, freedom and hope.

So, I will bow down before Him,
broken, blessed by everything He has done for me.
I will receive Him in all His Glory and
be eternally grateful for His unconditional acceptance of me.

Oh, what a God! How divine! How kind! I will love Him forever.
His thankful daughter forever I'll be.

Isn't God wonderful? What a mighty, holy, loving God we live with. If you do not know Him yet, please ask Him into your life and let Him love you.

Years ago, God placed these desires in my heart, and I wrote these thoughts down in my diary around April of 1987:

> My heart speaks to my Lord God, what awesome power is in that name! How grateful I am that this awesome power that comes from knowing God has been and continues to be at work in my life. His mighty hand leads my life, His eye watches over me, and He directs my steps and leads me in paths of righteousness.
>
> His name is to be lifted up. There is none like Almighty God! This creator Jehovah God has blessed me with a wonderful husband and three dear children. My life is full of purpose, and my existence has meaning—to live to the praise of His glory. To give Him my life, a living sacrifice, that will have a sweet smelling aroma, acceptable and pleasing to Him is my desire.
>
> He reigns in majesty and power, and His ways and thoughts are high above the earth so far removed from me. What a joy when, in His love, He gives me insight and wisdom into His ways. He alone is worthy, and He alone holds all things together. His name is great and deserving of all praise. At His name alone every knee shall bow. To know Him is to love Him and to love Him is to serve Him. I will follow Him as long as I live.
>
> Everywhere I look His grandeur, His greatness, His beauty is displayed. From the powerful, huge mountains to the vastness of the ocean waters and their beautiful white foamy waves that glisten in the sun. In the sweet melodious twill of the many birds—God is overwhelming in all His Glory. For He surrounds us with His love and even indwells us—oh the wonder of it all! "Oh Lord, our Lord how excellent is thy name in all the earth, who has set thy glory above the heavens! When I consider thy heavens, the work of thy fingers the moon and the stars… What is man that thou art mindful of him" (Psalm 8:1, 3&4)?

Now come with me to September 8, 1987, and look at another writing as my soul spoke to the Lord our God:

> Praise God for His love. He is so gracious, so merciful, so patient, and so faithful. He continues to show me His love through His care of Danny, Jennifer, and David, my children. Their lives are in His hands, and He is setting their paths. I am so grateful. Learning with God through the teaching power of the Holy Spirit is overwhelming, difficult, and deeply satisfying. I pray that the Lord will continue to lead me, guide me, teach me His ways, and direct my paths. I could not live a second without Him. It is amazing that such a holy, pure, righteous God loves me, and I am so glad it is true. God has used a sprained ankle to demonstrate His love for me. He is in charge—I am not. It is with a peaceful contentment that I know nothing happens in my life that is not allowed by Him.

September 11-13, 1987:

> Here I continue to sit. God continues to be in control. There is a burden being laid on my heart and I want to be still so I do not miss what Jesus is doing. God loves me. He continues to deal lovingly, gently, but firmly with me as I still find myself sitting, waiting for my foot to heal. I realize the things I have for so long trusted to God in my mind are now being put to the test. In my mind I have always agreed obedience and service to God are not in the things we do. It is different when it actually touches my life. Sitting here not being able to do anything, I have realized I had not really separated the two. I have felt disobedient and not pleasing to the Lord because I am not doing anything and I have let others' thoughts and opinions affect me. "How must it look to them? I am not really so hurt." Convicted by the Holy Spirit and overcome by God's love, I know pleasing God is not in

the doing, but in the knowing and worshipping of Him. Psalm 99:5 & 9, "Exalt the Lord our God and worship at His footstool; He is holy. The Lord also desires me to look to Him only—not husband, children, or friends—but Jesus only! A precious thought, that I, the creation of God, can bless Him and cause Him delight. "Bless the Lord, O, my soul and all that is within me, bless His holy name." Thank You, God for being so good!

I share my diary only so you may see that what God begins in you and me, He brings to completion. God, by His love and the inner working of the Holy Spirit has been moving me along and directing my paths from day one.

My heart has always longed for Him, and He has lovingly used my breakdown in depression and all my hurts to bring me to this place of totally abandoning myself into Him, of being able to totally receive His goodness and love as the answers for my great needs and longings. He has brought me to this place where I would finally let go and jump off the cliff and abandon myself into His adventure for me. He has caused my heart to love Him and to long for Him by the life of the Holy Spirit within me.

I know God is awesome, and I am safe and truly finding my home in the arms of my God. He has a story for each one of His children. I hope you are connecting with Him and allowing Him to work out His plans and purposes for you. He is the one and only God that we can count on, who will never let us down. Trust Him with all your heart today.

As I was learning to trust God with more of my heart, He was teaching me more about faith. Faith. Faith is exciting. It is choosing to believe in what cannot be seen. Then God takes it from there. Actually, God has had it all along, because faith is born of God. He created us with the need to place our faith in Him, and He enables us to believe. Our faith originated with Him when He formed Adam and Eve. Faith is not dependent on me once I choose to believe. It is released to God—no matter how limited—to God who is limitless, who can take that faith as a grain of mustard seed and grow it, move mountains with it, and use it to glorify His name in all the earth. This is what I believe He did for me when I was so sick that all I could do was to acknowledge His love for me.

God asks us to believe even in the face of no evidence. Faith for healing—let's suppose it depends on our faith. Then I could say, "Look, I had enough faith. I have been healed." Who gets the glory? Faith has all to do with Almighty God. I get no credit. God is the Healer—God alone—not the faith, the ability to believe. The focus is God and placing our faith (the faith born of Him) in His sovereign hand. God alone moves heaven and earth to answer prayer, not me. I only choose to believe like Abraham, Moses, and others who believed God as illustrated in Hebrews chapter eleven.

Although healing in our eyes may not be immediate, Jesus is always at work in our lives even when it is not as we may desire. The real questions are: Am I accepting whatever God allows into my life as long as He is glorified? Do I desire Him to be glorified above all else? Am I really sold out to Him and Him alone? Do I want Him just for Himself or for that and also what He will do for me? Is healing secondary or primary? Are God's will and purposes more important to me than being healed? These are important questions. The answers will reveal the truth of what is inside the heart. I have had to answer some of these questions in my own relationship with God about what He has allowed into my life.

I believe God desires me to seek Him and Him alone. He desires all my heart. He wants me to implicitly trust Him, to

A Leap of Faith

follow Him, and to believe in Him when it seems foolish to do so. I believe He wants to glorify Himself in me as I choose to accept whatever He desires in my life. Can I do that on my own? No! That is why Jesus indwells me. I need to draw on His strength and allow His name to be lifted up as I rest in Him. Who am I to understand God and His ways? Who am I to figure out why some are healed and why some are not healed? Isn't He the Potter? Am I not the clay?

God has laid the foundation, given me the blessings of His love, and the assurance of His care; now I will take this leap of faith. What an amazing God! How could I say no? I have thought about turning back because my little, dusty self still struggles with the bigness of God. So I am thankful that He is a patient and loving Father who doesn't give up on me but continues to love and encourage me along. He is constantly reassuring me that "I can do all things in Christ Jesus who strengthens me" (Philippians 4:13). I have only God to thank as together with my husband we place our hands in God's hands and ask Him, "Lord, what is our mission?"

Chapter 15

Lord, What Is Our Mission?

As God's new call on our lives was becoming stronger, I wanted to be directed by the Lord for a Scriptural basis for this new ministry. We had not received direction regarding a name of the ministry at this point.

I remember very early one Sunday morning asking God for His specific leading regarding a Scripture from which to develop a mission statement as the foundation for this new ministry. I was clearly directed to Isaiah 61 and after reading, meditation, and prayer, I felt very drawn to verses one through three:

> The Spirit of the Sovereign Lord is on me, because the Lord has anointed me to preach good news to the poor. He has sent me to bind up the brokenhearted, to proclaim freedom for the captives and release for the prisoners, to proclaim the year of the Lord's favor and the day of vengeance of our God, to comfort all who mourn, and

provide for those who grieve in Zion—to bestow on them a crown of beauty instead of ashes, the oil of blessing instead of mourning, and a garment of praise instead of a spirit of despair. They will be called oaks of righteousness, a planting of the Lord for the display of his splendor.

In the days to come, this Scripture would become very precious to us. God was imprinting those words deep on our hearts. As I shared this Scripture with Joanie later that morning, we both were in agreement that this Scripture would be the foundation on which this new ministry would be built.

The date was November 11, 2001. I came across a statement that I wrote in my journal that went hand in hand with what God was doing in our hearts: "Because we have been found, we have a mission to seek the lost." God has given so much to us at the great cost of the life of His Son, and we are privileged to give to others as freely as we have received. The next day I wrote in my journal:

> This Good News is for *all people!* "Anyone who calls on the name of the Lord will be saved" (Romans 10:13). "And how will anyone tell them without being sent?" That is what the Scripture means when it says, "How beautiful on the mountains are the feet of those who bring good news, who proclaim peace, who bring good tidings, who proclaim salvation, who say to Zion, Your God reigns!" (Isaiah 52:7). We are being "sent out" Oh God! Raise up an *army* of partners both in prayer and in finances. I was blasted away with 1 Corinthians 4:19: "The Kingdom of God does not consist in talk but in power." It is all God! Praise the Lord!
> Richard Foster wrote:

Lord, What Is Our Mission?

> The Good News must come in the power of God. No smooth words, no easy clichés, no enticing gimmicks! All slick image-making advertising campaigns are an offense to the Gospel.[1]

As I was being led by God during these early days of the formation of this new ministry, I purposed within my heart (Joanie fully agreed as well) that we would not resort to any human hard sell tactics, pressure, or manipulation of people for finances, prayer, or to become part of this ministry team. We would present our needs to God, share a newsletter with our partners in ministry and trust our Lord to provide.

The gospel of Jesus Christ stands alone entirely on the merit of the finished work of Christ on the Cross of Calvary. Any persuading to be done in the hearts of men would be done by God.

Human compassion can take on many forms. It became one of our goals, as God would provide, to help others around the world with humanitarian aid. Another form of compassion is the sharing of the Good News that we have joyfully received about our Savior with others. Foster writes: "If therefore we do not commit ourselves with urgency to the task of evangelization, we are guilty of an inexcusable lack of human compassion."[2] As we become more in love with our Savior, we will sense a greater urgency to share this great love with those who have yet to become free through His gift of life available to all who would come to God through salvation in Jesus Christ.

Our true heart of compassion causes us to give away God's love as we have so graciously received it from Him. Foster continues:

> The hungry can be fed. Millions can be reached with the message of life in Christ. He, whose power is over all, desires to use his people as agents of change. We are to walk cheerfully over the face of the earth, conquering evil with good in the power of the Spirit.[3]

Agents of change, what a marvelous calling! Can you imagine the curiosity that would overtake millions of people without Christ as they watched the believers' faces and actions all over this globe? Could it be that my God was calling me to really live above my circumstances? Might my reactions to the same life stresses all of us face be used for His glory to point others to Christ? This indeed would be a challenge I would come to embrace in the days to come.

What if all those who claim to truly know Christ and claim to have been changed forever by Him really lived that way by the power of the Holy Spirit? This next quote from Mr. Foster really impacted my heart both as a warning and as a reality check:

> The Good News must be backed by integrity in our lives. We cannot proclaim his love if we close our hearts to the hungry. We cannot proclaim his salvation if we have not been saved from our own greed. Flamboyant, prosperous Christians are an offense to third world peoples by their insensitivity to poverty and human deprivation, whether they come as traveling evangelists or sightseeing vacationers.[4]

Oh God, keep me broken before you *every day of my life!*

As God's mission was unfolding in our lives, we were being prepared to minister from a simple lifestyle ourselves. To relate to others we became unattached to things and attached to God and His love for people. All people!

Lord, What Is Our Mission?

Let's take a detour from some of the heavy things we have been considering and look at some items of praise from my journal dated 11/15/2001:

> Praise God! Today as I was going to our post office box, I wondered if a ministry gift would come for the new ministry calling in our life. We received a twenty-dollar Publix gift certificate as our first gift toward this new ministry and life of faith in our Lord. We decided to save it until we moved to Tampa as a symbol of God's provision in a new place. Later this afternoon, we received a call from someone asking where to send a gift as the donor is waiting for our incorporation to send it on. Both were unsolicited. Praise God. He is working. God has provided all four officers, two board members, and a staff member thus far. Great is Thy faithfulness.

I must at this point share a story that was a turning point during these formative days of our mission becoming more defined. I will never forget this day that I learned an important lesson from God about myself.

On November 20, 2001, I went out for a few miles walk that was a normal part of my routine. While on this walk, I sensed a nudging to share with a man coming in my direction that I was about to pass. I believe God spoke to my heart saying, "Ask the man if he knows Jesus." I did not share with the man as we simply smiled at each other as we passed. I became very convicted within my spirit and on returning back I confessed my disobedience to God and asked God for another opportunity.

I could not find the man, and then I saw him and waited for him to come closer to me so that I could talk to him. I asked him, "Do you know Jesus Christ?" He said that he believed in Mother Nature and really did not want to pursue the conversation. I smiled and told him that God loved him, and I continued to walk home. God spoke to my heart as I had a great peace come over me. The Holy Spirit very tenderly told me that the reason He prompted me to share with that man was not primarily for that man's benefit but for a test of my obedience to God.

God desires me to know His voice so that as He speaks to my heart more often, I will obey and not question. He confirmed in my heart that day that my concern should not be with the response to the gospel, but with whether I was faithful to His prompting to share. Wow! Did He get my attention? Most definitely! I committed myself to be obedient to His prompting and not be put off by fears or questions. I praise God for the personal way He deals with us as His children. He may do this in a different way for each of us, but He does deal with us. I will say, "*Yes, Lord!*"

A key piece of God's direction was granted on December 27, 2001. We found out that we were now incorporated in the State of Florida under the ministry name of: Alive In Christ Ministries, Inc. We were so blessed to have this name. Our theme verse from this name would be taken from Ephesians 2:4-5a: "Because of his great love for us, God, who is rich in mercy, made us alive with Christ." We would now be praying for many people by God's grace to be "Made Alive In Christ."

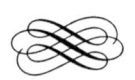

Living in Christ Jesus is life more abundant than I could have ever imagined. There is no boredom here. I am on an adventure with God. What seems so amazing and incredible to me is the expected and natural course of events for my God. I believe that this is the very way He expects us to live our lives when we receive Him in all His fullness into our hearts as our Savior and Lord. It is so amazing to me because it is so beyond what I could imagine.

That makes complete sense since it is exactly what Christ told us in His Word, 1 Corinthians 2:9, says, "...No eye has seen, no ear has heard, no mind has conceived what God has prepared for those who love him." Ephesians 3:20, says, "Now to him who is able to do immeasurably more than all we ask or imagine..." This is what God is telling us, and He wants us to have these things in our lives.

I would like to share a couple entries in my diary with you that speak to some of the thoughts God was speaking to my heart during this time as He was revealing His mission to my husband and me.

On October 20, 2001, I wrote this:

> I woke up at 7:00 this morning with what I believe was a conversation with the Holy Spirit. As He directed my thoughts to God, I heard Him tell me that many people would come to know Him through my life. I feel I must share God's love with my chiropractor and ask him to consider Jesus in his life. I have also felt led to stand up more in who I am in Christ Jesus in boldness and in power as my husband spoke a word for me today from God. Thank You, Jesus.

On November 19, 2001, I wrote:

> I went to my prayer team ministry to have a time of prayer for the needs of the church. During this prayer session, God revealed to me that I am to do a teaching in the church on the Holy Spirit. I am willing to let God use me in this way although I am nervous because I have never done anything like this before. I feel like I am going from the kitchen to the pulpit, and I cannot help but

think of how God chooses the foolish things in the world to confound the wise. He is amazing!

On December 22, 2001, I wrote:

I am learning to live in Jesus Christ my Lord and my Savior as the Holy Spirit enables me. It is new to me; it is deeper than I have been living. This new living is letting Him lead me and speak to me at the point of my need, the place where my heart is my inner self. I am realizing what it means to live in my desires and my wants, not in rules and regulations. I am walking more deeply in what He taught me years ago during my reconstruction from depression. It is freedom and fullness of joy. I do not find myself running along in this. I find that I am stumbling and falling a lot, but the Lord God is patient, and He is lovingly helping me and gently moving me along. I am wiped out by this knowledge that God will enable me to speak and share of Him, His life, His salvation, His love. In Christ, I will do what He asks me to do and go where He asks me to go. He will enable me and I will live what He has taught me in His Word. To God be the glory, great things He hath done!

On January 7, 2002, I wrote:

Yesterday, I spoke on the Holy Spirit as God told me to do. It was a blessed time. God did a mighty work in my heart to bring me to this point to be able to get up in front of people and speak a teaching on the Holy Spirit and His work in our lives (and experience it at the same time). I thank the Lord for what He did for me to enable me to share and for the blessing He gave to us all. I am looking forward to what God is going to do with us as we move to Tampa.

These entries reveal some of the work God was doing in preparing me to enter into a new phase of ministry. He used these days to stir up my world and cause me to move on with Him. He was leading my husband and me into a new call with a new mission. My heart had to be moved beyond the world I had known and enlarged to include a more aggressive role in ministry. God definitely had my attention, and I was cooperating as He spoke to me through my prayer times, Bible reading, and in my thoughts as I went about my daily routines. As my husband and I prayed together and God spoke to our hearts, we placed ourselves before Him and He gave us the formation of our new mission. We knew that God desired us to minister in a completely different way, and we would need to incorporate under a ministry name. God gave us the name Alive in Christ Ministries and placed a desire to reach out to people in ministry who need to be refreshed and renewed in their own lives. God used Isaiah 61:1-3 to give us our direction and purpose as a new ministry.

In placing ourselves at God's disposal, my husband and I found ourselves on the road again.

Chapter 16

On the Road Again

Before continuing with this story I must stop to ask you a question. Is it possible that, as you have been reading this account of God touching two people's lives, you are wondering, "Who is this God, anyway? I do not know Him in a personal, intimate, and loving way. Can I really be forgiven of my sins and know that I will spend eternity with Him?" I must say, "Yes."

You can really know God in such a close and intimate way. Take some time and read the account of His love in the Gospel of John. See for yourself how real, compassionate, and forgiving Jesus Christ is for all who would come to Him. I am not talking about doing things for God but coming in our emptiness to God. He is waiting, if by faith, you will call out to Him. There is no one like God who will come into your life and make you a whole new person on the inside. Then what is happening on the inside will affect your relationships, your integrity, your decisions, and your way of thinking. You will be set free from your sin and made alive by His power. He cleanses, heals, restores, and refreshes. Our God is real, alive, and powerful yet tender, and He desires to love you and be loved by you.

He is not a set of rules and regulations but the Creator of the universe who has given freely of His Son Jesus Christ on the cross two thousand years ago, so that you and I could know God in a deep and personal way. Please consider this life-changing decision, which will have an impact on your life both now and for all eternity. All that we have shared with you is true. God is awesome, and He loves you more than words can describe.

2 Corinthians 5:17 declares: "Therefore, if anyone is in Christ, he is a new creation; the old has gone, the new has come!" He will make you new if you come to Him just as you are. Ask Him to forgive your sins and He will enter your life as your Lord and Savior.

If you have not made this wonderful, lifetime commitment to receive Jesus Christ into your life as Lord and Savior, why not stop and by faith believe and receive for yourself this gift of eternal life. Find a local church and pastor that can help you grow in Him as you read the Bible and pray to God. Your heart was made for God. He will bring forth in your life what an entire lifetime without Him could never accomplish. Read the words of Jesus as recorded for us in John 10:9-10:

> I am the gate; whoever enters through me will be saved. He will come in and go out, and find pasture. The thief comes only to steal and kill and destroy; I have come that they may have life, and have it to the full.

The choice is yours. Why not choose life?

On the Road Again

We soon came to realize we would be on the road again. Joanie and I prayed and decided to move back to the Tampa, Florida area. Our children would become part of our ministry team, and that area would become the home base for Alive In Christ Ministries, Inc.

We began to pray for the Lord to lead us in the sale of our house. We bought a sign and placed it out on the street. Several calls came regarding the house and some people came by to see it. We set our price within the range of what we would need with a little room for negotiation for a sale.

On December 4, 2001, we received a call from a real estate agent who saw our sign outside. Our sign was "for sale by owner." He proceeded to tell me that he already had someone who wanted to live in our neighborhood. He asked me, "If I bring you a buyer, would you pay my commission?" I told him that we did not want to go through a real estate agent because of the full commission and would sell the house ourselves. He then said, "The commission would only be three percent, and the buyer was anxious."

I was wondering how he could have an anxious buyer who had not even seen the house, was already qualified, wanted to be in our neighborhood, and could most likely close on the deal when we needed it to close. I thanked him for his interest and said no thank you.

Immediately after hanging up the phone, I became aware of what a unique opportunity I was letting go of while we were praying for our house to sell. I felt the Lord telling me in my heart, "Bob, there is something in this call. Let go of your pride. This man can help you."

I shared that with Joanie, and we decided after prayer to call the real estate agent back. We did not have his phone number or the full name of his company. We prayed and asked God to show us as we went to the white pages and a partial name came to our minds. We called and, praise God, it was the right office.

We would soon find out that he also was a believer in Jesus Christ, quite helpful, and most professional. I called him back and said, "If the buyer will give us our asking price, we will be happy to pay your commission." The commission was within the exact range of negotiation that we had allowed for to make a deal on a private sale without a real estate agent.

Within one hour, the real estate agent brought a buyer who loved the house and talked about all of the things she would do when the house became hers as she went from room to room. Then she went out into our front-screened entrance and spoke how she would like to put up a privacy fence.

A she left we knew God was working but He is *always* working. The real estate agent called us back that afternoon and at 5:00 PM that day we had a signed contract. I remembered my need to put aside my pride and get out of the way of what God was doing. The closing date we agreed to was exactly the day we wanted to move. They were even willing to adjust the time earlier so that we could get on the road with our move across the state.

God is good, all the time! All the time, God is good! We believed that another piece of His plan was now unfolding as God was doing things to prepare the way for us to be free from the ownership of things requiring our maintenance, so that we might be completely available to go wherever He leads, whenever He leads, to whomever He sends us. Thank You Lord that your ways are not our ways.

On the Road Again

I wrote in my journal on 12/9/2001:

> I was blessed with this portion from God's Word this morning: Job 19:25-27, "But as for me, I know that my Redeemer lives, and that he will stand upon the earth at last. And after my body has decayed, yet in my body I will see God! I will see him for myself. Yes, I will see him with my own eyes. I am overwhelmed with this thought!" Wow! To be with God at last! What a glorious thought! My heart yearns for this more and more these days!

The next morning, I related to the following Scripture more than ever before. I wrote:

> Even though I have read this many times before, my heart condition has come more in line with this truth at this time in my life. Praise God! He is all that my heart desires, and He is worthy of all of me! Galatians 6:14: "As for me, God forbid that I should boast about anything except the cross of our Lord Jesus Christ. Because of that cross, my interest in this world died long ago, and the world's interest in me is long dead." Oh my God, only You, only You, only You!

During these days of upcoming transition in preparation for our move to start this new ministry, I was getting more and more excited that this freedom I was enjoying was intended for all of God's children to enjoy. It is when we want Jesus so much that our focus becomes what His focus is and His will for our lives becomes played out in our joyful obedience to love and serve Him with great delight.

I was greatly moved by the following statement from John Eldredge:

> Notice that the people who aren't so good at keeping up with the program but who are very aware of their

soul's deep thirst are captured by Jesus' message. Common folk tear the roofs off houses to get to him. They literally trample each other in an effort to get closer to this man. . . . People act like this when it is a matter of life and death. Crowds trample each other to get out of a burning building; they press into the mob to reach a food line. When life is at stake and the answer is within reach, that's when you see human desire unmasked in all its desparation.[1]

To have such a burning, driving, passionate desire for Christ to "show up" in our lives will bring our wills, hopes, and dreams to a place of fulfillment found only in Him. This new joy and way of living was not readily understood or accepted by all whom I was sharing with; nevertheless, Jesus was real and working mightily within my heart, and I would continue to press on in Him.

How could I be so certain that God would open up Alive In Christ Ministries, Inc. for His glory? That was simple. It was His calling that was birthed in my heart, so God would be the One to bring this ministry, and the healing by His Spirit to needy people, in His time and for His glory. We were simply to move out by faith and trust God to do the work. As we packed our boxes, this assurance remained strong in the One Who gave this vision in the first place. So much had happened since that day in the prison when the Holy Spirit spoke to my heart to trust God alone for all that He would bring to pass.

At this point all I desired was life from above. I had been through programs, planning sessions, strategies, and promotions. Now I wanted God Himself to show up mightily in my life—and not only in my life but in all of His people.

This is too good to be kept in a way of small thinking. This is a universal need among His people. God, how will they know unless these two broken clay pots get out there in your world and tell them? We desire to live among them, showing the awesome, life-changing power demonstrated by God Himself.

As I wrote these words, my heart wept with both joy for what He has done and for the urgency of the hour for believers everywhere to be passionately in love with their Lord. This in and of itself would cause the onlooker to wonder what is going on among these folks.

That is how the truth found in 1 Peter 3:15 will become realized: "But in your hearts set apart Christ as Lord. Always be prepared to give an answer to everyone who asks you to give the reason for the hope that you have. But do this with gentleness and respect." You see, when we desire God above all else, others will take notice and some will desire God for themselves. Now that is not a program but a motivation for evangelism. They will ask because they are curious regarding what they see. You and I simply point them to the One, Jesus Christ, Who is the only true Source of our joy. Now that's exciting!

John Eldredge writes:

> Christianity has nothing to say to the person who is completely happy the way things are. Its message is for those who hunger and thirst—for who desire life as it was meant to be. Why does Jesus appeal to desire? Because it is essential to his goal: bringing us life.[2]

Are you really happy with the way things are? Are you really happy? I am finding out that my completeness is centered in Christ. I love Him passionately and desire to live for Him with all my heart as long as He gives me breath.

On December 30, 2001, a website was established by a good friend of ours under the address of:

www.aliveinchristministries.org. We were so grateful to God for this new addition to the ministry's outreach. We prayed that God would reach many for His Kingdom through this tool. I wrote in my journal entry 1/12/2002:

> Today we load the truck. Tomorrow is our last day at our current place of ministry. Monday we move to Tampa. Thank You Lord for the quick sale of our house. We trust You Lord to open up this ministry You have called us to in Your time, through Your grace, and by Your power. You are awesome (a word I reserve only for God), God, and I love You and trust You alone to do what You told me You would do. How and when You do it is up to You. I give You my availability and my heart.

I believe that only a life entrusted to God can be a life of adventure worth living. We moved on and relocated into an apartment and trusted God as our hearts were saying, "Here we are God, now what?" We desired to be faithful, knowing God would lead us step by step in the direction He wanted us to go.

God provided us with a godly board of directors made up of local professionals in the community who donated their time and resources and a good friend who was gifted in helping us to sharpen our focus in the vision God had given us.

We were so blessed by God as He brought people our way who had great strengths to come alongside areas of our need. Isaiah 8:13 was very special to my heart during this time: "Do not fear anything except the Lord Almighty. He alone is the Holy One. If you fear Him, you need fear nothing else."

As we proceeded along in establishing our new calling, I had to submit yet another area of my life completely to God.

On the Road Again

I have chosen to be very vulnerable with you, our reader, in this account because I want you to be assured that this process of growth was both difficult and yet most necessary. The following account in its entirety is shared from a very personal struggle I faced. It had to be given over several times until God won out, and I received the victory in a marvelous way. This journal entry is dated 3/27/02:

> Psalm 37:5: Depend on the Lord, trust him, and he will take care of you." God, I confess to You this morning that I have often been very anxious regarding our financial support. I have often looked to the post office box and our personal mailbox and wondered, *Where is the support?* Please forgive me! Are You not the One who called us into this ministry? You are the One who will provide! We have funds for now and as they continue to go down, may I depend on You more and not on these funds. I need to grow in faith in this area and see *You alone* as our Source and Supply! Please free me from any appeals through manipulations of the phone, letters, or e-mails. Thank You for this morning's Scriptures. I will read Psalm 37. Psalm 37:3-5: "Trust in the Lord and do good. Then you will live safely in the land and prosper. Take delight in the Lord and he will give you your hearts' desires. Commit everything you do to the Lord. Trust him, and he will help you."
> Psalm 37:7: Be still in the presence of the Lord, and wait patiently for him to act." 11: "Those who are gentle and lowly will possess the land; they will live in prosperous security." 17b: "The Lord takes care of the godly." 19: "They will survive through hard times, even in famine they will have more than enough." 25,26: "Once I was young, and now I am old. Yet, I have never seen the godly forsaken, nor seen their children begging bread. The godly always give generous loans to others, and their children are a blessing." 23,24: "The steps of the godly

are directed by the Lord. He delights in every detail of their lives. Though they stumble, they will not fall, for the Lord holds them by the hand."

Then I wrote *yes!*

Psalm 37:34: Don't be impatient for the Lord to act! Travel steadily along his path. He will honor you, giving you the land. You will see the wicked destroyed." 39: "The Lord saves the godly; he is their fortress in times of trouble." Thank You God for the comfort, assurance, and promises from your Word! You met me at my very point of need today! I will trust You Alone.

Shortly after that time I was set free from looking to what I thought would be the method of God's provision as I put my entire trust in Him alone!

As I follow God in our new call, I, Joan, find myself having to move again. I arrived in this place that we had lived for these past couple years with a feeling that I was just passing through, so my roots had not gone down too deep. I knew God had definite purposes for bringing my husband and me to this church, and I was glad to be a part of the ministry here. I would miss some very special people that had become my friends, and that would make leaving difficult. I don't like good-byes, and this place had a church full of folks I loved very much. We had laughed together, cried together, and prayed together so we had a very strong bond, and our hearts are still together even though miles separate us.

I continue to be amazed by how lovingly God prepares His children for things He will do in their lives. Years ago, I remember having a devotional time while my children where in school in which I had felt impressed to give all I had to God. It was such a special time of praying and telling Him that I loved Him more than anything or anyone on earth. I told Him I didn't want to have anything between Him and me. I truly wanted Him to be Lord of my life. I gave Him my heart and all my earthly possessions. I told Him He could have my furniture, my house, my clothes—everything. I would stand before Him with nothing, and I would give Him me. If I lost everything for whatever reason, I wouldn't care if I still had God.

I want Him to be my satisfaction and the love of my life. I wanted to be sure that nothing was standing in the way of giving Him my all. I felt God's presence envelop me, and a peace and contentment filled my heart. It was an exercise that needed to be done to make sure I didn't make my possessions more important than my love and commitment to God. Little did I realize that God would use this in a very real way in my life years down the road.

Now this memory of giving God everything has came back to me as I prepared to move. God had my heart ready to give all my earthly possessions away if that is what I needed to do in order to go wherever He would lead us. So as I packed up our belongings and gave some furniture and stuff away, I felt peace. I have ended up with more than I thought I would keep, but God is not finished yet and I am ready to give it all away. I am smiling at how good God is, for when I think I am giving up, He only blesses me more. Why hold on to what I cannot keep anyway? I only receive what I can keep forever in return, which is God's love, His indwelling presence, His peace, and His confidence. The saying" we cannot outgive God" is so true.

As I write this all down, I am overwhelmed by what a great and mighty God you and I have. I feel so loved, so safe. I know that as we moved to Tampa to establish our base of ministry, God has gone before us and prepared the way.

We rented a wonderful apartment. We were near our children and our grandchildren, and we are blessed. I no longer see the things I have given up; what could I give up for God? Everything I have is all His anyway. I see blessings all around me. I see Him fulfilling His desires for the people and me. He wants to love and bless and encourage as we let Him be our hands and feet here on earth. What a privilege to live for God! We take our marching orders from Him.

My daughter's baby has turned one year old, and we got to be at the party! My son and his wife have two children, and their little boy will turn one on September 19, 2002, and, God willing, we will be there at his birthday party! My youngest son is in the air force and keeps in touch with us as much as he is able. I am blessed beyond measure, and I am thankful to God.

Sometimes we wonder what the days ahead hold with all the terrorism threats around us. Our circumstances don't always make us feel safe, and that is just exactly why we need to place ourselves in God's protection. He is greater than our circumstances.

He needs to be our focus, and as I have learned this and have applied it to my life, it has made all the difference in the world. When I have to be on the road again or in the sky in an airplane, I don't have to be fearful because my life is in the hands of God, and only what He allows to happen to me will happen. I have learned to trust Him completely, and if I do get fearful, I run to Him for He is my Refuge, my High Tower, and a very present help in time of need.

I love Him, and I believe now more than ever that He will always be there for me. I could never leave my country, my children, or my things if this weren't true. I know that God is helping me to do this because in myself I do not have the ability.

God will help you do what is in your heart. He is greater than your darkest fear or your worst nightmare. Please remember that. When your hope is in the Lord God, you will be safe in His care.

I have no idea what will happen to me when I fly to other countries or go traveling in my own country, but I know who is committed to taking care of me—and that is my Father God. When I need help, comfort, or peace, He will give it to me right at my point of need and not a moment sooner or later. I can count on Him.

This world is not our home; we are just passing through like the song says. When our delight and satisfaction are found in the wonder and love of God, then we don't have to be taken up with the things of this world. We realize that all we see will one day burn up. Our life is in Christ, and our joy is in Him. One day we will see Him face to face. Knowing this and living this in our hearts makes us satisfied.

Chapter 17
Satisfied

To be brought along to a place in one's life where God alone becomes your satisfaction is truly a blessing. To know He is speaking to your heart and that He means more to you than any other person, plan, or purpose that you would choose, leads to the road of intimacy with God.

He became my satisfaction in life. Whatever would come my way would not be in my control. My response to whatever comes my way is certainly my choice. I would come to understand more clearly during the winter and spring of 2002 how much my entire satisfaction in God alone would carry me through days of uncertainty while I remained quiet before Him in prayer and obedient to His directives in my life.

One morning after praying with my pastor and one of our elders, we were watching a brief video clip that the pastor would be using as a part of his presentation the following Sunday. Jesus was speaking to the disciples who had been fishing all night and still came up empty. He said to them, "Go out deeper and cast your nets on the other side of the boat." Peter's response was "If you say so, Lord." The waters in the video became filled with fish, and at that very moment I filled up with tears as I sensed the Holy Spirit saying to my heart, "I am preparing you for a mighty ministry in the days ahead. You and your wife are right where you need to be."

Those first two months in Tampa were very quiet days of preparation for the groundwork for the ministry that God was preparing us for in the future. We would continue to trust Almighty God for whatever He would desire to do through us in the days to follow. I was at complete peace and filled with anticipation for whatever He had in store for our ministry team. Yes, I said, "ministry team" as we were now praying for God to bring others to this ministry.

To become content in God and whatever He allows coming my way and provides for in my life has given me great satisfaction:

> But godliness with contentment is great gain. For we brought nothing into the world, and we can take nothing out of it. But if we have food and clothing, we will be content with that. People who want to get rich fall into temptation and a trap and into many foolish and harmful desires that plunge men into ruin and destruction. For the love of money is a root of all kinds of evil. Some people, eager for money, have wandered from the faith and pierced themselves with many griefs. But you, man of God, flee from all this, and pursue righteousness, godliness, faith, love, endurance and gentleness.
> (1 Timothy 6:6-11)

There are many choices that we have in life. It seems that many people only believe that they have one choice—

that being the accumulation of more and more things will satisfy their desire to have enough. We do have another choice that is most freeing as it is practiced. This choice is to desire less. This may not sound very profound, but the change that it has brought about in our family has been a welcomed breath of fresh air. We are finding that as God becomes more involved in our lives we desire Him so much that things that used to be important have dropped away without our even missing them.

So many people are moving through this life so fast that they are missing the present. I used to be one of those people until I began to learn to live in the moment. God has so much to say, so much love to give, so much fellowship to be enjoyed if we would simply slow down enough to take hold of all that is ours in Jesus Christ.

God Himself has placed us in a wonderful position to be loved by Him. As we take delight in His Person, we find great satisfaction in that relationship, which will last forever—long after the things we have acquired in this life will have rotted away. We were created to love God and glorify Him forever; therefore, our heart's desire can only find fulfillment in Him.

As I came to accept the gifts God has given to me, both in His provisions for my needs and in a growing, personal relationship with Him, my response developed into one of gratitude and satisfaction.

I believe that a life of contentment (which is a choice by the way) is at peace with life's circumstances. It's indeed a most wonderful and apparently rare state in which to live! This is true freedom—to accept from the hand of God His care and provision, to enjoy the beauty of His creation, to love Him and be loved by Him, and to have people in one's life to bless and be blessed by. What more can a forgiven, restored, healed, and renewed person ever desire?

God Himself is my desire. My love for Him has increased my capacity for my love for Joanie. Our love for each other has grown stronger and more beautiful as God became more of the central focus of our marriage. Those who have experienced this first hand can attest to the truth of what I have just described. When our perspective on life has eternity in view, we value people above things.

Jesus gave His life for people. Jesus invested all that He had in people. Jesus had compassion on people. We are gifts to one another. Do our chosen priorities reflect such an attitude? Why not consider making a mid-course correction today if this is not the case. God can do wonders with a willing heart!

Have you noticed how boredom seeks out continual entertainment and yet is never fully satisfied? Why? Only God Himself can satisfy! I thank my God that He has made a wonderful provision for me in my relationship with Him. It is in this relationship alone that I am fulfilled, at rest, complete, and satisfied. I am so thankful that our God does not bring up my past but leads me on into this present moment with great purpose and meaning. The future is all His and I continually place my confidence in His competence. Living in the moment has brought great satisfaction into my life. I would like to encourage you by asking you to meditate on the truth found in these beautiful words written by Helen Mallicoat:

> I was regretting the past and fearing the future. Suddenly my Lord was speaking: "My name is I AM." He paused. I waited. He continued, "When you live in the past with its mistakes and regrets, it is hard. I am not there. My name is not I WAS. When you live in the future, with its problems and fears it is hard. I am not there. My name is

not I WILL BE. When you live in this moment it is not hard. I am here. My name is I AM." [1]

On the morning of April 2, 2002, I was very blessed through the reading of Isaiah chapter fifty-five. As I read verse 2: "Why spend money on what is not bread, and your labor on what does not satisfy? Listen, listen to me, and eat what is good, and your soul will delight in the richest of fare," I said within my own heart once again, "Only God can satisfy." I continued to read and meditate on the whole chapter of Isaiah fifty-five and then I wrote in my journal:

> This morning I had a fresh encounter with my Lord as I shared my desire to be God's friend. So much of my prayer life to this point has been for God's power or God's anointing on behalf of ministry concerns. I smiled and told God that I loved Him and simply was blessed to be His friend. It was a most delightful time in the presence of my Abba Father.

I will never forget that moment as I looked up and had the widest smile on my face. Tears of joy streamed down my face as I was caught up in the wonder and amazement of God's love. Think about this, to be a friend of God and not just to seek Him for what you want but also to seek Him because you enjoy Him and He enjoys you. Now that's a relationship! I trust that by now you are getting the point that when God is your satisfaction, you are truly satisfied beyond your wildest dreams.

Throughout this story I have shared both peaks and valleys. There are times in our lives when we think we may be over something, and yet we may have the need to give areas over to God again. I am including the following account to make you aware that struggles continue along the way while great things are happening. The good news is that God remains faithful though our ups and downs.

I wrote the following journal entry after being very discouraged at the end of a day that I needed to confess to my Lord my need to focus on Him alone *once again!* 4/30/2002:

> I had a difficult time in my quiet time as I needed to repent and ask God and Joanie to forgive me for yesterday's conversation while we walked. Once again, I had looked to people, the post office box, and at the lack of what I had set up by my own human expectations for this ministry and the support it needed. Once again, I was directed in brokenness back to God alone. When will I get it that He is my Source and Supply. I feel like a failure in this "faith walk" as I want so much to trust Him alone and not look to any person, organization, or anything in the place of my Heavenly Father's provision for us. Lord, thanks for your patience with me. I love You and need to stay rooted in You and Your call upon my life and this ministry. Well, all I can do is start over, be quiet, and watch God work. There really is no better place to be. Praise the Lord!

God continues to be my satisfaction and the delight of my heart. As I change, He remains the same. He can be trusted. He can be counted on. He is holy, just, righteous, loving, and forgiving, but what really puts a smile on my face is that He is my friend!

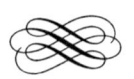

It is wonderful freedom to learn that God is our satisfaction. It is also wonderful for me, Joan, to realize that when

Satisfied

I was dissatisfied, He didn't change, I did. I need to look inside myself and find out why I am discontented.

There are times when I cannot keep up with the things God has shown me. I may feel weak or overwhelmed by my circumstances and I do not feel victorious. It is at these times I must remind myself that God is still the same; He did not change. There is a problem within me, and I must take time to examine my ways and thoughts and find the trouble spot.

I cannot walk perfectly at all times. I find that the joy of living with the Holy Spirit is in knowing that He is there. When I am having trouble with issues in my life, people disappointing me, or feeling discouraged because there isn't enough money to meet the bills, the Holy Spirit is within me. His life is still close and real. To feel or not feel His presence does not mean He went away. Sometimes He is quiet, but He is there.

It is in these situations that I must remember I am satisfied with God. I may have to become still myself to hear God's still, small voice, but He will guide me and help me in my circumstance as I turn to Him for help. Feelings must never be my indicator of His involvement in my life. He is helping me even if I feel that He is far from me. When I am in the pit, He is in the pit with me. When I feel alone, He is right by my side. He told me He would never leave me or forsake me, and when trouble comes He is there.

God has proved Himself over and over to me, and I know that when I need Him, He will be there for me. His love for me is limitless, and He will move heaven and earth to help me. Nothing will keep me from His care. In my trials, in my stress, my soul can cry out to Him, and He will hear me. Not only will He hear me, He will send His angels to care for me.

As I have allowed God's love to heal me, He has become my satisfaction, and He has shown His love to me by restoring my heart and life. I have hope and confidence in God, which is the evidence of His power and love working in me. Too long I have tried to live a good life by doing the right thing to get God to love me. Wrong! I have His love and in Him I have everything I will ever need. I have learned that He cares about the littlest thing that touches my life. If it is important to me, it is important to Him. He cares. When my life hit bottom, I found out how great God is because He was there at the bottom with me. My Father God held me while I bled and opened my eyes to see the truths that set me free and healed my broken soul. I view my life in Him totally satisfied that He is my Shepherd and He will lead me where I need to go. I am happy that I have put my hand in His hand and that I am allowing Him to lead me. When life gives way around me, He is my rock and I will stand firm in Him. He is my satisfaction.

As God has led my husband and me into a closer walk with Him, we have grown closer and share a deeper intimacy with one another. We feel safe with each other. We have enjoyed deeper times in the Word of God together as He speaks to our hearts through the Bible and prayer.

On one such occasion, God brought a change into our lives. One Sunday morning we decided to stay home and share some quiet time together. The day before had been very busy. As we were praying together, the Holy Spirit took over and marvelously spoke to our lives. I began to praise the Lord for His greatness and tell Him that we desire His name to be lifted up at all times. During this time, the Holy Spirit spoke to Bobby's heart and asked him if he would be willing to give up preaching and begin ministering in the quiet places (to the wounded hearts of people).

Bobby said yes to God and gave up his heart's desire. As we continued praying, God impressed on my heart this question, "Is your all on the altar?" I realized it was not. I realized I desired to stay in the quiet places, the background, and my comfort zone where I had been all my life. I had to give this up to God, and I told Him that if He wanted to use me in the public places that I would go there. It was difficult but necessary for me to put this area of my heart on the altar of sacrifice to the Lord. I had to lay down the strong "I" in me.

As we shared with one another, we realized God had asked Bobby to give up the public places, the pulpit, being upfront with people, his comfort zone where he had ministered all his life, and to go to the quiet places. He had asked me to give up the quiet places to go to the public places. As we prayed and thanked God for what He had shown us, God assured Bobby that since he was willing to do this He would give Bobby many opportunities to preach and minister. We thank God for His love and mercy. It is amazing and wonderful how He deals with the deep places of the heart.

I know I must hold nothing back from my Lord and through these experiences I have learned that He will bring important areas of my life to my attention and help me put things in order so that I may be fitted for His purposes. It comforts me to know that God will not ask of me more than I can give Him. He will take me just as I am and use me—the woman He created me to be—His workmanship. He will use my personality and fit me in the Kingdom of God where He knows He can use me best. I can rest in the love of my heavenly Father and know that He will use all that has happened in my life for His honor and glory.

That is why I believe nothing is lost and even the painful times are redeemed in His loving hand. Not only is this true, but no matter how awful life can get and no matter what I have to endure, God will bring beauty from the most ugly situation and work miracles of kindness and love from the most painful places life can take us.

I continue to struggle even though I have acknowledged this awesome care of God in my life. There are times when I am scared and full of questions. When this happens, I go to my knees and find strength and help in my hour of need. If the particular trial is too difficult, I find I have to speak the name of Jesus over my soul with each breath that I take—for there is no other way that I will make it. His presence is comforting, and He will show up at just the right time. He has never let me down. This is God, and only He can do that when we let Him have His way in our lives.

God has done all He can do to get the message through to us that He loves us with an everlasting love; that He wants us to let Him pour out His love on us. I hope you will bring Him all your hopes and dreams, all your cares, pains, wounds, and bruises and let Him love you and heal you and "restore unto you the years that the locust have eaten" as Joel 2:25 says. This reveals to us the type of God we serve and His desire for His children to flourish in their souls as He protects their lives.

We cannot always understand why certain things happen the way they do. I don't know why God didn't keep me from experiencing depression and that is not the point of my writing this book. I believe that I will know what God wants me to know, and the rest I have to leave with Him. If I struggle with questions that I cannot have answers to, I keep myself from moving on and experiencing God's love and healing. I would rather use my mind and my energy in letting God bring healing into my situation, than waste myself on questions I may never understand.

I think life will always have its struggles and pain, and I would rather spend my time going in the direction I can receive answers than wasting my time trying to understand why this or that happened to me. I choose to place myself in the arms of Almighty God and let Him make sense of my brokenness and restore me. My heart doesn't have all the answers, and there is so much I cannot understand, but knowing the One who is sovereign and in control allows me to leave the difficulties with Him and find satisfaction in His loving care. What do I have to fear when God is on my side? My hope is in Him!

As God alone continues to become our entire satisfaction, we fall more and more in love with Him. That is why we believe that intimacy with God is our primary privilege in life. As our Loving Father has graciously restored us, He has put within our hearts a fresh desire to love and serve Him with renewed passion.

Chapter 18

A Renewed Passion

I would like to introduce this chapter with a quote I found along the way in my reading. I do not know the source, and I am not the one who wrote this. I simply pass this on for your consideration: "People of passion will desperately pursue what the educated tell them can't be caught!" This is where the rub comes by comparing each other's experiences. Simply because someone else has not seen or experienced something, does not mean it cannot be attained.

As my passion got stronger I had to depend on God to enable me to see things by faith in His promises, His timing, and through His power. As we were still praying and receiving counsel regarding the need to focus our attention on what our primary calling was to be, I did a word study on our ministry Scripture that had by this time become a regular part of our lives, prayers, and practices.

> The Spirit of the Lord is upon me; because the Lord has anointed (to consecrate) me to preach good tidings (to be fresh, to carry) unto the meek (depressed in mind, needy, especially the saintly); he hath sent (appointed) me to bind up (to wrap firmly, healer) the brokenhearted (to break into pieces, crushed, hurt, quenched, broken in feelings, will and intellect), to proclaim liberty (freedom, spontaneity of outflow) to the captives (those taken away), and the opening of the prison (jail delivery) to them that are bound (those harnessed) to proclaim the acceptable (delight, favor, good pleasure) year of the Lord, and the day of vengeance of our God; to comfort (to console, to ease, to have compassion) all that mourn; to appoint unto them that mourn in Zion, to give (to restore, to bestow) unto them beauty for ashes, the oil (to lavish richly) of joy for mourning, the garment of praise for the spirit of heaviness (feeble, obscure, darkish, dim); that they might be called trees (strength, support) of righteousness, the planting of the Lord, that he might be glorified.
>
> (Isaiah 61:1-3)

As you can see from a study of this Scripture, the care, healing, and restoration of broken and needy people is very close to the heart of God. After several weeks of prayer and godly counsel, Joanie and I would seek to follow the Lord's leading for Alive In Christ Ministries, Inc. We believe that the following mission statement clearly describes the primary calling of Alive In Christ Ministries, Inc. "Encouraging people in ministry who need to regain their passion and empowerment for Christian service." We desire to minister among those who minister to others. God is using our past experiences, hurts, and healing to reach out to others with the hope and encouragement of our Lord. We have a deep love for people in all types of ministry to be encouraged, restored, and renewed.

I had new opportunities to preach and those times flowed from a heart of freedom, love, and compassion. God's people are very loved by God, and I am now privileged along with my wife to come alongside them. As we share the impact of what He has done for us, we encourage others to trust Him completely to work in their lives.

God was stirring something new within my heart that I would like to share with you from one of my journal entries:

> Today while in the shower, I was impressed with the thought that just as Joseph was oppressed for his dreams and preserved by God, while misunderstood by those around him, God used him to preserve God's people for the future. I believe that God spoke to my heart that regardless of what may come my way by opposition, persecution, or rejection, God would use me to prepare His people for the trials that will come in the future. This is major spiritual warfare, and God is the Victor. What others may mean for evil, God will use for good.

As our passion for God and His Kingdom strengthens, He prepares us for trials, testing, and ultimate victories. I am growing to understand more and more that God enjoys our fellowship, loves to exchange intimacy between Him and us, and gives to us what we need according to His timetable as we rest in His sovereignty.

In Romans 5:3-5 we read:

> Not only so, but we also rejoice in our sufferings, because we know that suffering produces perseverance; perseverance, character and character, hope. And hope does not disappoint us, because God has poured out his love into our hearts by the Holy Spirit, whom he has given us.

Throughout the history of Christianity, God has brought about some of His greatest work through man's deepest suffering. One of the greatest impacts that are made on a new believer is that God Himself works a mighty change in the character of that new believer. The transformation is often so extreme that those around such persons cannot help but stop and take notice.

History records such dramatic changes in the characters of people such as St. Augustine, John Newton, the apostle Paul, the disciples, and countless others whose passion for God far outweighed the former passions.

A changed life is often accompanied by persecution and conflict. Why? Those who formerly knew such persons would rather have had them remain as they were since the new believer's changes toward God remind their friends of what is needed in their own lives.

It all comes down to whom you trust. Psalm 20:7 states: "Some trust in chariots and some in horses, but we trust in the name of the Lord our God." Psalm 23 reassures us that God Himself is the One who restores our soul. Psalm 33:4 states: "For the word of the Lord is right and true; he is faithful in all he does."

You may be wondering at this point why I am so passionate about God. Who else is there worthy of the very best that you have to give? Who has satisfied your heart to the fullest like Him? Who has forgiven your sins and healed you beyond any human comprehension? Who has purchased a place in heaven for you eternally because of the work of His Son, Jesus Christ, on the cross of Calvary? Who else is there that can take you as you are and change you forever by His grace and love? I say only God can do such wonders, and that is why I am so passionate about my love for Him. Is it possible while you are reading these words that He is drawing your heart back to Him or to Him for

A Renewed Passion

the first time? There is no other Savior! There is no other King! God Himself passionately wants all of you as He has given all that He had to give in Jesus Christ for you.

I would like to leave you with a great hope to enable you to press on in this life and remain faithful unto God to the end. What is waiting for you is so much better than what you have experienced in this life. Remember who you are in Christ if you know Him and what you can become in Christ if you will today give your life completely over to Him.

You are His child. You have eternal worth and value. Jesus already paid the price for your salvation. You and I some day soon will be shedding all we have down here as those of us who have been forgiven by God through His Son Jesus Christ will live with Him forever. Let your passion be renewed as we are told in Philippians 3:20.21:

> But our citizenship is in heaven. And we eagerly await a Savior from there, the Lord Jesus Christ, who, by the power that enables him to bring everything under his control, will transform our lowly bodies so that they will be like his glorious body.

Don't just hang in there until He comes! Be passionate about God! Serve Him with all your heart. Love those around you for Jesus' sake until they ask you why you love them so much. Give your best to God with each day that He has entrusted to you. Learn to be a steward and not an owner for all things come from God's gracious hand. Enjoy Him and let the beauty of Jesus Christ radiate from your life. The closer you get to God, the greater the impact will be on other people for God. My prayer for you is to have such a renewed passion.

As my husband and I trust God with every detail of our lives, our hearts have been drawn closer to Him and this has renewed our passion. Life in Jesus Christ is to be lived with gusto, vibrancy, with all our hearts. I cannot straddle the fence, which means I am sometimes living my own way and sometimes living Christ-like. Christ wants all my heart, and there is no room for mediocrity. He wants me to be sold out to Him. Christians should be the most alive, most enthusiastic, people on the face of the earth and I want to be full of joy because of Jesus Christ in me the hope of glory! Jesus came that I might have life and that more abundantly!

My heart has not always been passionate about Jesus. I went through many years of dutifully loving Him and doing the right thing. I believed with all my head that He loved me, but it was not in my heart.

I loved God but in a way that had to earn His love. I realize now that it was one-sided and lacked the joy and passion Christ desired for me to have in a dynamic relationship with Him. When I realized that Jesus loves me, just me, I started on the road to really knowing joy and peace in God. I am reminded of John 12:24 where Jesus says, "I tell you the truth, unless a kernel of wheat falls to the ground and dies, it remains only a single seed. But if it dies, it produces many seeds."

Once again, this makes me realize that nothing is lost when Jesus Christ walks into your life and touches your broken heart. All that died or was crushed in your soul is brought to life by His touch. His direction will bring much fruit and bless many lives. After all, look who is holding your broken heart. Who better to put your life in order than your Creator? He will not just pick up the pieces and put you back together, He will make the pieces new and vibrant. He'll put you back together with passion for Him in your soul.

God loves you and me. I want you to get this thought with me—if I never do another thing for God for the rest of my life, if I just sit here in this chair and love Him, this is all right with Him. I do not have to earn His love. Finally God was getting my attention, and the barriers I had erected through years of pleasing, obeying, and earning were crumbling down. The love of God was flowing into my heart and soul, and I was able to know freedom and receive the love and acceptance that had always been mine since before the foundation of the world, (Ephesians 1:4).

Now I could own the truth that He wants me and that He will never love me more or less by what I do or say. He loves me just as I am. He loves you just as you are. Please let this truth flood over you and heal your soul. This is for all of us who have believed that we have to work hard to please God or get His attention. Good news: We don't have to work hard! Jesus says, "I love you, just the way you are. Come, be with me, share your heart with me."

I know this is true. It has changed my life with Jesus from duty to delight and given my soul renewed passion.

The wonderful changes that God brings about in our lives are not for us alone. We are to live for the praise of His glory. God's love keeps coming toward us. Our love for Him is manifested in the way that we love one another. As we walk by faith in Jesus Christ and trust Him completely to lead the way, we joyfully follow His call on our lives to an ongoing adventure.

Chapter 19

An Ongoing Adventure

One Sunday in our church, the pastor had a picture up on a television monitor of people in the front car of a roller coaster. The caption over the picture was: "The Ride of Your Life." He spoke that morning about our lives being directed by God.

As I kept looking up to that monitor, I thought over and over about our ongoing adventure with God. He is surely taking us along on the ride of our lives as we have placed ourselves entirely at His disposal. The ride has not stopped yet, and although there are peaks and valleys, this ongoing adventure with God is incredible.

He has proven Himself faithful countless times. As Joanie and I have taken a leap of faith, it has not been a blind leap into the darkness. It was a leap of trust into the outstretched arms of Almighty God. He is our Provider, our Protector, our Peace, and our Sustainer.

God equips those He calls and brings to pass eternal changes in the lives of those He touches. We are being transformed into the likeness of God. What a thought! Read these words from 2 Corinthians 3:17,18:

> Now the Lord is the Spirit, and where the Spirit of the Lord is, there is freedom. And we, who with unveiled faces all reflect the Lord's glory, are being transformed into his likeness with ever-increasing glory, which comes from the Lord, who is the Spirit.

Along the way in this ongoing adventure, I am learning that our position in this life is of no consequence to God. He will perform great and mighty things through the life of anyone who will depend on Him. If God can work through us, He certainly can work through you! The key to having a servant's heart is found in the example of Jesus Christ while here on earth and spending much time with Him daily.

I agree wholeheartedly with Isaiah 2:22: "Stop trusting in man, who has but a breath in his nostrils. Of what account is he?" Since God's strength carries us, why not admit your weaknesses to Him and move out of the driver's seat and enjoy the ride. It will truly be the ride of your life!

I have found the following statement to be true more times than I can count. I do not know the source of these words but see for yourself if they are true: "Almost anything of any importance in your walk with Christ is discovered on the way to somewhere else." I have seen this happen so often. God reveals more of what He desires to do through me as I faithfully walk in obedience in all that I know.

When we are in dark places in our lives, we must hold fast to the truth revealed previously by God through the light of His Word. Remember that God's blessing on our lives is not limited to our present circumstances or difficulties. During this adventure, we must put aside our timetables, our past experiences, and our limitations. The One Who

An Ongoing Adventure

is timeless, limitless, and fearless is leading us. He can be trusted!

I am so thankful that God blesses what He originates. This is so contrary to our way of planning through our agendas and then at the end asking God to bless our plans. Why not try this novel idea and hear from Him first. He will not go against His Word. He does bless abundantly that which He initiates. He sustains what He creates, and He finishes what He begins. I want to go where He is going. What about you?

The amount of difference that God will make through your life into the life of another is directly proportional to the difference you have allowed God to make in your life. God has so much for us if we would but believe Him to do all that He has promised. Hold on to your seat as you read a glimpse of this truth from 1 Corinthians 2:9: " ... No eye has seen, no ear has heard, no mind has conceived what God has prepared for those who love him."

Psalm 25:4-5 described the prayer of my heart on 5/05/2002:

> Show me the path where I should walk, O Lord; point out the right road for me to follow. Lead me by your truth and teach me, for you are the God who saves me. All day long I put my hope in you.

At that point, I wrote the following account in my journal:

> This is my prayer O God! I woke up this morning specifically asking You, my God, for Your directions and a preview of the future days of ministry. Please speak to my heart! In prayer, I believe that God spoke to my heart saying, "I am about to open the windows of heaven for

you! You are an obedient servant and as opportunities come up for ministry, after prayer and believing you are to go, say *yes*. Don't look to what you have for I will provide for you! I will bring glory to My name."

God was continually preparing us to trust Him for each new day and to walk through doors of opportunity that He would open for ministry.

We went away for a week of rest and preparation for the ministry trip to Taiwan. During that week (in which this book was begun), I had some beautiful times with my heavenly Father. Joanie and I enjoyed rich times together as we simply rested in His love and our love for each other. I am choosing to share one of my more personal journal entries dated 5/17/2002:

> I prayed and asked God to speak to my heart again this morning. After reading *Yes, Lord* (a book about God's provisions for one of His minister's in ministry), I was spoken to in my heart: "You will go from place to place, and I will provide for you in ways unexpected and in ways that you would not anticipate it to come. I love you. You are my sheep, and I am your Shepherd. I will care for you!" Then I was overwhelmed, and I wept because of God's love and promise. We will move around the world and receive from His Hand what we need when we need it. Thank You Lord!
> Psalm 78:23-25: But he commanded the skies to open—he opened the doors of heaven—and rained down manna for them to eat. He gave them bread from heaven. They ate the food of angels! God gave them all they could hold!
> Praise God! You will do this for us! I am finally getting it! Our Abba Father desires and is waiting to give! We must ask and ask specifically with a pure motive! May I come to You, Abba, more often for all things!

An Ongoing Adventure

A whole new dimension in my life of prayer was opening up for me. I was taught by a fellow pastor whom I pray with weekly the importance of asking God for favor with people and situations, and for open doors of His choosing. I began along with Joanie to praise God for those whom He had already prepared to be favorable toward us in ministry. We continued by faith to ask Him more often for favor in specific situations and would trust Him more than ever for each day's provisions, protection, and the fulfillment of His promises. God is good, all the time! All the time, God is good!

This brings this chapter of our journey to a close. God is faithful! We have accepted an opportunity to minister to those serving on the mission field in Taiwan at the end of June 2002. We are looking forward to the next phase of God's new call bringing us into a walk of faith and love with our Lord. Now we are here in Tampa, having heard God's call on our lives to prepare for this ministry, now known to us as Alive In Christ Ministries, Inc.

Thank You Lord for leading us this far and for those who are partnering with us in this ministry. We love You Lord!

> To him who loves us and has freed us from our sins by his blood, and has made us to be a kingdom and priests to serve his God and Father—to him be glory forever and ever Amen! Look, he is coming with the clouds, and every eye will see him, even those who pierced him; and all the peoples of the earth will mourn because of him. So shall it be! Amen. I am the Alpha and the Omega, says the Lord God, who is, and who was and who is to come, the Almighty.
>
> (Revelation 1:6b-8)

I, Joan, would like to share with you an invitation to join your adventure with God. God loves you. He longs for you, your company, and your friendship. He wants you, He desires you—your heart, the essence of who you are, all of you. He is your Creator. He knows you better than you know yourself. He has given all to capture your heart. He is your Lover, your Friend, your Comforter, your Father, and your Mother. You are not alone. He has promised to never leave you nor forsake you. He delights in you, and you are in the palm of His hand. This is why God doesn't want you to just have lots of knowledge about Him; He wants you to experience Him.

God gave His Son Jesus Christ to die for you—to take your punishment on the cross. His love for you redeems you, keeps you safe, guides you, and provides you a place in heaven with Him for all eternity. God gives the Holy Spirit to dwell in you—to guide your heart and mind—to lead you and thus fulfill those marvelous plans and purposes He has for you. By the Holy Spirit's life in you, you and God may develop a close, intimate relationship.

You were created to fulfill the dreams of God with all the marvelous hopes and longings that go along with those great dreams. He gave you the dreams, and He wants to see you live your adventure—the reason He created you. God is everything you will ever need. He is your satisfaction. With Him, all things are possible. He has given you an adventure with a mission to fulfill and, as only God can do, He makes sure you are equipped and totally given success (as He views success). Certainly, the way will be full of potholes, and you may stumble, but you will never completely fall. You are marked for success, but only if you *give up*—give up trying to calculate the risks and give up trying to be in control.

This adventure requires total abandonment of your heart and soul into the totally, loving Lord God Almighty. Are you willing to turn over your heart to Him? Are you willing? God is waiting. He will never force His love on you. He will never force you to live His plan for you. He waits for your answer. This is part of the wonder of God—He waits for you to say yes. Your cooperation unlocks the door and sets the plan in motion. Think of it! The God of heaven, our Creator, does not override your will. He chooses to wait and that is the *key* ingredient to this marvelous life. God wants us to want Him. Our time here is a life of intimately knowing God and walking with Him hand in hand—hearts knitted together as one.

It is so true that when you give Him yourself and banish all your hesitation—when you place your hand in His—then your adventure can begin. He is looking and longing for the heart that desires Him above all things. You will never know what is on the other side of the door until you open it up and don't just peek in but walk through to the other side.

He will provide for you, and your heart will know rest and peace—for your longings and your dreams have found their home. Your heart in the Heart of God, your Father. Go and live your adventure.

Now it is your turn to join hands with God and live for the praise of His Glory!

Chapter 20
Now It's Your Turn

As we prayerfully considered the reason for sharing our story up to this point in our ongoing adventure with God, our primary motivation was to encourage *you* to draw close to Him and trust Him completely with all your life, which must start by trusting God with all your heart. What God has done thus far and will do for Joanie and me in the future is His plan for our lives.

Now it's your turn to consider being totally sold out to Him! What will you do with the promises of God? Will you believe Him to the extent of acting on that belief? Will you say, "Well, that was a nice story in their lives, but God would never show up in my life." Why not? Our experiences may be very different, but our God and His great love for us is the same.

This is what unites each of us together in the Body of Christ. It was His Blood that was shed for all our sins. It is God's Holy Spirit that works in us to bring to completion in our lives that which He began (Philippians 1:6). God desires for His children to take Him at His Word, love Him with all of their hearts, share that love with the people He brings in their paths, and watch Him work in marvelous ways.

Will you be one of those people? The choice is yours. He has already prepared the way for you through the sacrifice of Jesus Christ, His Son, for you.

I have shared with you a gift that was costly, but I believe most necessary, in the design of this book. That gift has been vulnerability wrapped up with the covering of complete honesty. Why have I chosen to share such very personal thoughts, prayers, and experiences with many people I will never know this side of heaven. It is because God directed me in prayer to share this way so that you would be encouraged. In your times of lacking faith, needing forgiveness, and having to get back to the basics, may you believe God to be Who He says He is and become a child once again—as I have had to do so frequently.

I trust that as you have unwrapped this gift you have done it with your own sensitivity and looked honestly into your own heart for the answers to the questions God has asked of you. You are very special to Him, because God gave Jesus Christ so that you could live with Him forever.

Now, what are you going to do with the rest of your life in response to such a great gift from our awesome God? That answer, in time, will determine to what extent you really believe God to work in your own life. Don't just try Him. Immerse yourself in Him! You will never be disappointed!

God is still involved in changing lives today. He will take anyone who comes to Him and enable him to live a higher quality of life by His Spirit than could ever be attained or hoped for without God. How can I be so sure that this is true? "Jesus Christ is the same yesterday and today and forever" (Hebrews 13:8)

So many people today try to live their lives so they will be remembered after they are gone. How about considering something far greater than leaving your mark in this world? God will take a life submitted to Him, and through that life, make a lasting impression on others for eternity. A lasting legacy continues as it flows out from those lives that have been surrendered to God. This legacy for the glory of God is found in the lives of changed and forgiven people who will spend eternity with God because His children shared His love and an opportunity for salvation with them.

Consider this challenge: "Live so that when people get to know you, they will get to know Christ!" Christ is what matters, and He gives us the opportunity to be a part of God's eternal plan in living out full, exciting, and purposeful lives for His glory among people needing God's redemption. One of the great things about God is that He is no respecter of persons, regardless of their age or status in this life. God can use you right here and right now regardless of what season of life you are in along your journey. He has no limitations and simply looks for our availability.

As Joshua was encouraging the children of Israel to keep the commandments that Moses had given them, he told them: "… to love the Lord your God, to walk in all his ways, to obey his commands, to hold fast to him and to serve him with all your heart and all your soul" (Joshua 22:5). This is great advice for us today as well. Stay close to the One who has changed your life forever. Be loyal to God who has set you free. Give all your heart to God who loves you immensely.

Remember this truth from God's Word throughout your journey in your walk with Him: "The Lord delights in the way of the man whose steps he has made firm; though he stumble, he will not fall, for the Lord upholds him with his hand" (Psalm 37:23-24). God remains faithful throughout the bumps in the road of life. God cares about all your life. Now it's your turn! Go with God all the way. Abide in Him along the way. Enjoy Him forever as He shows you His way. Go ahead and take a leap of faith as you trust Almighty God to carry you along for the ride of your life!

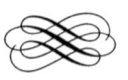

I, Joan, would like to look with you at Psalm 8:1, 3-5:

> O Lord, our Lord, how majestic is your name in all the earth! When I consider your heavens, the work of your fingers, the moon and the stars, which you have set in place, what is man that you are mindful of him, the son of man that you care for him? You made him a little lower than the heavenly beings and crowned him with glory and honor.

Isn't this wonderful of our Lord God? My heart is blessed and rejoices in the goodness of God and what He has given us because of His great love for us! We don't deserve to be treated so extravagantly and trusted so highly with His mighty creation, and yet He has given us this privilege.

My desire in writing this book has been that you would realize even more than you do already how much God loves you and wants to be involved in your life. His Word is full of His love for you, and He gave us His love letter to encourage our hearts and tell us His love stories and life-changing truths.

I pray that you will go before His throne with boldness and thanksgiving and allow Him to fill your heart with Himself. You are precious in His sight. He wants you. He has shown me through my own life that He desires to use ordinary people like you and me to glorify His name in all the earth. He has been doing that since the beginning of time.

Look with me at the people He has used to bring glory to His name. There was Noah who built a huge ark because it was going to rain. He had never seen an ark or rain, but he did as God told him and through him the world was started again. Then there is Abram whom God called to leave his country and go to a land that was foreign to him. God began the Jewish nation through him. There is Moses, who couldn't speak well and offered God every excuse not to use him to free His people. God used him to lead His people to the Promised Land. We meet David, the shepherd boy, who defeated a huge giant named Goliath and who later became king of the Israelite nation. God placed a woman named Rahab in the line of David that eventually included Jesus, our Lord and Savior. God called a young, unknown, woman, Esther, out from among her people to be placed in the king's palace and become queen in order to save her nation at the risk of losing her own life. What do all these (and other people that I have not shared about but are there in the Bible) have in common? They all believed God, trusted Him in the face of the unknown, and obeyed Him, putting their lives on the line for Him, and He came through every time. God has used the unknown people, the people the world would not consider great or worthy of greed deeds to do impossible things for Him.

God is a great God, and He will continue to use regular, everyday people to silence the arrogance of people who think they are great and powerful. He has a plan with a purpose, and He will see it accomplished.

The question is will you and I get on board and be a part of God's plan? I think the best part about being involved with God is He loves you; He will watch over you;

He has prepared the way for you, and the end of the story is victorious—life everlasting in a place called heaven that is beyond our wildest dreams. All He asks of us is to believe and act on our belief. This brings God the greatest joy, when we show Him by our actions that we believe Him, that we trust Him. He will work on our behalf to do what cannot be done if He didn't help us.

Let's stop trying to make Him fit into our plans, and let's fit into His victorious plans. He loves you. I have no idea what goes on in your world and what you have to face, but I do know that God is there for you. Find Him for yourself in the midst of your greatest difficulty; find what He has for you. Don't settle for the world's lies and deceptions any longer. Take your leap of faith with Him and live the life He has for you.

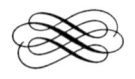

Well, there you have it. Thanks for coming into our lives through reading this testimony of some of the things that God has been doing in our lives. We have appreciated the time that you have taken to get to this point in our story. Now it's your turn. What has God been saying to you? What areas of your life is He waiting to be surrendered unto His Lordship? Will you take a leap of faith into the outstretched arms of Almighty God? Whatever He calls you to do will never be greater than His calling you to intimacy with Him. Give yourself completely to Him and enjoy the ride of your life. You have been prayed over by both of us.

We have shared many words but none are greater than the Words of God. Therefore we pray for you the same prayer that the apostle Paul prayed over the church in

Now It's Your Turn

Ephesus. God bless you as you love Him and consider what you will do with His Call on your life:

> For this reason I kneel before the Father, from whom his whole family in heaven and on earth derives its name. I pray that out of his glorious riches he may strengthen you with power through his Spirit in your inner being, so that Christ may dwell in your hearts through faith. And I pray that you, being rooted and established in love, may have power, together with all the saints, to grasp how wide and long and high and deep is the love of Christ, and to know this love that surpasses knowledge—that you may be filled to the measure of all the fullness of God.
>
> Now to Him who is able to do immeasurably more than all we ask or imagine, according to His power that is at work within us, to Him be glory in the church and in Christ Jesus throughout all generations, forever and ever! Amen.
>
> (Ephesians 3:14-21)

Endnotes

Chapter 3. What Went Wrong?
[1]. Andrew Murray, *The Ministry of Intercession* (New Kensington, PA: Whitaker House, 1982), 67.
[2]. *The Daily Bread*, RCB Ministries (Grand Rapids, MI 2001), Day 58.

Chapter 5. Coming Apart At The Seams
[1]. "Slow Me Down Lord."

Chapter 8. Joy Restored
[1]. Charles S. Swindoll, *The Grace Awakening* (Dallas, Texas: Word Publishing, 1990), 5.
[2]. Ibid., 5,6.
[3]. Guido Kuwas, "New Christian Miraculously Saved from Death and Shame", Global Revival News, (12-17-01).

Chapter 11. Back To School
[1]. Reggie McNeal, *A Work Of Heart* (San Francisco, CA: Jossey-Bass Publishers, 2000), 58.

Chapter 12. Summer Struggles
[1]. Reggie McNeal, *A Work Of Heart* (San Francisco, CA: Jossey-Bass Publishers, 2000), 58.

Chapter 14. A Leap Of Faith
[1]. Warren W. Wiersbe, *Real Worship* (Grand Rapids, MI: Baker Books, 2000), 164.
[2]. Brennan Manning, *Lion and Lamb* (Grand Rapids, MI: Chosen Books, 2000) 123.

Chapter 15. "Lord, What is our Mission?"
[1]. Richard J. Foster, *Freedom of Simplicity* (New York, NY: Harper Collins Publishers, 1998), 214.
[2]. Ibid., 211.
[3]. Ibid., 208.
[4]. Ibid., 214.

Chapter 16. On The Road Again
[1]. John Eldredge, *The Journey of Desire* (Nashville, TN: Thomas Nelson, Inc., 2000), 39.
[2]. Ibid., 43.

Chapter 17. Satisfied
[1]. Helen Mallicoat, "I AM", Taken from "Listen For The Lord", © 1977 Hallmark Cards, Inc. (Kansas City, Missouri) SBN 87529-519-3 Internet Resource.

To order additional copies of

A LEAP OF FAITH

Have your credit card ready and call:

1-877-421-READ (7323)

or please visit our web site at
www.pleasantword.com

Also available at:
www.amazon.com
and
www.barnesandnoble.com

Please contact:
Alive in Christ Ministries, Inc.
PO Box 340405 Tampa, FL 33694-0405
Website: aliveinchristministries.org